A YEAR IN TEXTS

AN EXPLICIT READING PROGRAM

T 78367

KERRY GEHLING

PETA

Primary English Teaching Association

This book is dedicated to the memory
of Thomas Gehling.

First published November 2000

Copyright © Primary English Teaching Association 2000
        Laura Street, Newtown NSW 2042 Australia

National Library of Australia Cataloguing-in-Publication data
Gehling, Kerry.
A year in texts : an explicit reading program
Bibliography
ISBN 1 875622 39 X.
1. Reading (Primary). I. Primary English Teaching Association (Australia).
II. Title.
372.41

Cover design by Stephen Goddard, Stephen Goddard Design

Text design by Anna Webster, Oracle Desktop Designs

Content consultation by Joelie Hancock

Edited by Barry Gordon

Contents

Acknowledgements

I am indebted to Joelie Hancock, who has worked with me to develop my writing and programs to the point where they could be presented for publication. I thank her for her help and expertise.

I am also grateful to Di Schafranek and Julie Astill for their support and their useful and challenging ideas.

My thanks also to Michael Gehling, who makes the computer do what I want it to do, and to all my family, who have supported me in finishing this work.

Chapter 1: Program practices

Emma stands proudly in front of her classmates. Her mother is here, too — the significant adult in the audience. With an air of satisfaction, Emma explains that she is proud of her work. She has learned new ways to investigate a book — to study it in depth. One of those ways, she says, is to set questions.

Emma now realises, she tells us, that books have issues that are interesting to study. She explains that her "time management" has been good; she has used a "priority listing", and has been able to work steadily throughout the term to achieve her goals. It is the end of term 3, and Emma is using a new language to describe her reading approach and practices.

The reading study in my classroom continues to equip and empower readers like Emma, and attracts positive comments from students and parents alike. The wide-ranging objectives, assessment structure and activities in my reading program are able to captivate and enthuse students; in turn, they are respected and appreciated by parents.

The year's program is structured around the analysis of different texts, with a focus on explicit communication of expectations, tasks and assessment criteria. I have refined this process over the years and I now feel well pleased by the outcomes my students are achieving, and by the enjoyment they show in their reading.

When parents tell me: "He's reading so much more now!", and students say: "I always found books really hard to choose, but not any more — there are so many that have been recommended by the class", I am convinced that the explicit nature of the teaching lessons, along with the negotiated programming and assessment, are meeting the needs of the students I teach.

Reading aims

Each year, together with my class, I construct reading assignments that aim to:

◆ encourage students to read

◆ encourage a wider choice of reading material

◆ encourage students to develop an interest in what their contemporaries are reading, and to use the views and recommendations of others in selecting their own reading material

◆ develop specific reading and viewing skills

◆ develop students' ability to read and view critically

◆ develop time-management skills.

An Explicit Reading Program

All these aims are built upon the framework of the national English statement and profile. Teaching and learning is planned around specific outcomes from the profile.

The practice of explicit teaching

A number of theories and strategies have reoriented my teaching over the last ten years, and I now consider it a necessity to make explicit what will be learnt and assessed. Much of this practice is underpinned by Luke and Freebody's framework of the 'four roles of the reader', and the questioning models of Bloom and Wiederhold (see chapter 2). Comber and O'Brien's approaches to critical literacy have further influenced my practices in developing students' ability to interrogate texts.

My approach to assessment is firmly based on the authentic assessment models (see chapter 2, p 20). These models foster students' abilities to work according to known and/or negotiated criteria. The important consideration here is that students are able to use their involvement in their own assessment to develop control of their learning. As they do, they better recognise the integral part that assessment plays in learning. Explicit teaching practices — goal-setting, instruction and establishment of performance criteria — are critical in enabling this process.

Year overview

The general plan for each year is organised around assignments — one for each term. These assignments address the broad aims of the program and are tailored to the specific needs of each class.

Term 1

Students complete a general assignment requiring them to read a variety of books and to complete a variety of associated tasks. This is an introduction to the assignment format, and does not have the targeted focus of the following terms' assignments.

Term 2

This assignment focuses on an author study. Students read and comment on books by chosen authors. In addition, they complete a research study about one selected author.

Term 3

This assignment is based on one book. Students select a book that is challenging to read and is 'meaty' — a book with depth. The book choice must be discussed with, and approved by, the teacher. The study is then based on questions (expressed as tasks) that the students set for themselves. This is supported with explicit teaching about questioning.

Term 4

Students study media texts drawn from magazines, television and newspapers. The study does not usually include a major assignment; the focus is on the development of critical understandings.

This is a basic outline. Each year brings something different, and the structure should be revised continuously to meet the needs of the new group of individuals in the class.

Advantages of a year-long program

This program is designed to build throughout the year, both in the depth of content explored and in the independence with which students carry out their investigations and demonstrate their developing skills. It reaches a climax in the third term with an in-depth book study and a completely negotiated assignment. The last term is quite different, involving media texts and working towards developing students' critical capabilities.

Students respond to this progression, gradually becoming more confident in discussing a variety of contemporary issues, expressing opinions and identifying the purposes and intended audiences of texts.

Each assignment contains tasks that build on existing skills and understandings, as well as tasks that require students to move forward in their thinking. Any new skills are identified and taught explicitly. In all, the assignments provide a structure that enables the students to move from the known to the unknown.

The flexibility offered by this program means that it can be used in a variety of situations and for a variety of year levels. It can be incorporated within various units of work or can stand alone as a reading unit. Tied with explicit teaching, this pattern of assignments can be tailored to fit the needs of different groups of students and can be managed by teachers with a variety of experiences.

As they build from one assignment to the next, students build their learning — developing skills in reading, viewing and writing. They are able to choose much of their own writing, and are guided to generate questions and criteria that support their choice of reading material. The flow of activities enables students to build their skills of time management, supporting them in controlling their own learning. Because they must produce texts for a variety of audiences, students have meaningful goals to aim for in meeting assignment deadlines.

Age range

This program is targeted at the middle-school age range — Years 6–9. It can, however, be used with younger students, since learners will choose books at their own level.

Features

Whatever their age, students undertaking this program are supported by explicit teaching, training in time management, negotiation of their curriculum and knowledge of the criteria by which they will be assessed. These elements are all features of this program.

Throughout the program, a number of important practices are combined:

- involving the students
- communicating with parents
- using the library
- integrating information technology.

Each of these practices will be explored in what follows.

Involving students

Involved students are more highly motivated to make achievements of which they can be proud, and which make them feel that they are really learning. Student involvement will increase in response to strategies that encourage students to:

- sequence their assignments
- manage their own time
- negotiate the outcomes that they are to achieve
- investigate scaffolded questions
- reflect on their achievements so as to map further progress.

Sequencing assignments

Each assignment should include tasks that provide for a variety of learning styles. In part, this can be achieved by ensuring that student readers engage with texts in a variety of roles (after Freebody & Luke, 1990) and from a variety of perspectives (after De Bono, 1988). See chapter 2 for further discussion of these approaches.

While tasks are set out in an order that appeals to the teacher, students need the flexibility to investigate questions in whatever order they choose. The only requirement that must be set is that a question is not tackled before the teaching component for that question. The teacher needs to make clear the questions to which this requirement applies.

Managing time

Time management presents potential difficulties for all people. It is an area of organisation that can be supported by teaching, and by the provision of schedules and pro formas. Students need to be provided with:

◆ a due date, which is entered in a diary and communicated to parents

◆ a schedule, which is discussed and on view in the classroom, and is updated regularly

◆ dates for explicit teaching lessons, which are entered on the class schedule

◆ a pro forma for prioritising work and making a personal schedule.

Negotiating outcomes

When skills are taught explicitly, students become aware of what they must know and do if they are to achieve to a high standard. However, not all students are able to articulate the requirements for themselves. Others simply do not stop to think about them.

When a class of students expresses the requirements together and records them in chart form, a visual representation can be generated. Aided by this, students are able to set their sights on the level of performance that they require of themselves. This is one way of making outcomes explicit.

Investigating scaffolded questions

Since the assignments in this program are supported by explicit teaching, students are supported while they take control of their own learning. The assignments include activities that enable students to apply skills already learned. They also include scaffolded questions that allow new skills to be included within their repertoire. Thus students are able to consolidate their knowledge and skills, then draw upon this prior learning to make new achievements.

Reflecting on achievements

Throughout, students are required to reflect on their time management and the quality of their work. The class is provided with support in this endeavour through class discussions, posted schedules, individual conferencing and pro formas for timetabling.

At the end of each unit — and whenever they complete activities during the assignment — students are provided with space to consider their learning and outcomes. This gives each student the opportunity to reflect. For the teacher, it is an opportunity to set to rights any misunderstandings that have occurred, and to plan to avoid these in future teaching. It also allows the teacher and parents to gain insight into a student's thinking, providing a guide for moving students from the known to the unknown. Students are not often able to accomplish this review process without the support of explicit teaching.

Communicating with parents

Communication with students' parents is a vital part of any learning program. All parents wish the best possible outcomes for their children in whatever endeavour they undertake. Learners make better progress if their support bases have congruent values. As teachers, it is our responsibility to ensure that our plans and required outcomes are communicated to parents as explicitly as possible. The following methods of communication have proven themselves to be effective in supporting students throughout the reading program under discussion.

Letters

A letter at the beginning of each term informs parents of that term's expectations, helping to draw all of a student's support structures together. Not only does it ensure that parents are aware of their child's commitment, it underscores the belief that student, teacher and parent are a partnership of learning.

The start-of-term letter should outline the proposed program, explicitly indicating the kind of support from which the students would benefit, and requesting parental involvement when necessary. Follow-up letters can be sent towards the end of the term to inform parents of the term's outcomes and to invite them to joint celebrations.

Informed parents are more able to support students, and more likely to know and understand what is happening in their child's classroom.

Portfolios

A portfolio system is a regular means of communicating a variety of assessment tasks and student work samples to parents. The parental feedback it produces provides support for students and insight for teachers as they plan further work and scaffolding in explicit teaching.

Each assessment task included in the portfolio contains:

- an outline of the set task
- the intended outcomes (in clear language that is meaningful to parents)
- a sample of the student's work
- teacher comment — either in the form of annotations to a work sample or in a designated place on an assessment sheet
- the student's reflection
- provision for parent comment.

The portfolio is sent home at least once a term. The best timing is at the end of a unit of work, while the outcomes are still fresh in mind and the parent can be led through the work by a child who is excited, rather than one who says: "That was a long time ago". Parents may be overwhelmed by huge amounts of information — sending quantities home at the end of the term usually means that it is not read in detail, while information at the end of a unit captures their interest and ensures that they are kept informed.

Three-way conferences

Parent interviews can be a stressful time for teachers and parents alike. Each party worries about what the other will say, while the child sits at home or, even worse, outside the classroom, wondering what is being said. A three-way conference overcomes these problems.

In a three-way conference, the child is present at the interview, and helps to chair the meeting. This presents an opportunity to gain considerable benefit from the purposeful application of oral language skills, while the stress is minimal. Additionally, all interested people have input. The letter over, which is sent home to parents, explains in more detail a strategy which has produced outstanding results. More information can be gathered from the book *Together Is Better* (see references).

Dear Parent,

This year, interviews in 6/7G will be conducted as a three-way conference. This means that the interview will include your child, who will be part of the discussion group.

I have always felt that interviews should be times when students are able to enjoy the positives that can come from affirming their achievements, or gain the benefit of participating when problems are discussed. Often the first question a student asks his/her parent after teacher–parent interviews is "What did she say?". By being included, the student is not left in the dark, and a basis is set for further meaningful discussion.

In the conference, all the people who have an interest in the developing skills and attitudes of your child will be present and will have an input into the action plan.

If there is some matter that you particularly want to discuss without your child's presence, you are welcome to make an appointment.

I believe that a three-way conference is one important way to demonstrate to students that we positively support their learning. Inviting them to the conference shows the value that we place on their views and the respect that we have for their opinions. It also clearly demonstrates that, together, we will support their learning and celebrate their achievements.

Reports will be sent home this week and interviews will be conducted next week. Please indicate the three most convenient times for your family. I will do my best to accommodate your requests. I will send home the allocated time on the agenda for the meeting.

On the agenda you will find the topics I would like us to discuss. There is also some space for you to add items you would like included. Your child will have his/her own agenda, which will be part of the proceedings.

I look forward to meeting with you and your child.

Regards

Kerry Gehling

The kind of letter I typically send to students' parents in preparation for a three-way conference, held in the middle of the year.

Using the library

The resource centre is the source of most of the reading material used in this program. The teacher librarian therefore becomes a crucial support, and it is important to keep this person informed about the requirements that your students will have. Negotiate the involvement you would like, provide a copy of each assignment and include the teacher librarian in supporting students in the selection of their books. An introductory lesson — in which, together, the class teacher and teacher librarian discuss and display some books that may suitable — is a great support for students.

Students should be encouraged to make their own selections and to discuss these with either their class teacher or the teacher librarian. Student-to-student recommendations should also be encouraged after reading — a recommendation list can be a fixture in the classroom and can also be a support in the selection of books.

Integrating information technology

Information technology is a great support — for both student and teacher — in setting and developing the assignments in this program.

Student work may be presented in word-processed format. This mode of delivery should be negotiated with students — there should be no disadvantage to students who do not have access to a computer at home. The provision of extra time at the school computer is a successful way to overcome this problem.

It is particularly valuable to establish an individual database of the books read by each student throughout the year. This not only ensures that each student has the skills to set up and operate a database, it provides a running record of the material covered, and can highlight those books which have been found interesting. A database can also be set up for the whole class; this is useful as a recommendation list.

In the third-term assignment, students may choose to use the computer to:

◆ conduct book searches

◆ support time management and recording

◆ communicate with other schools/students about suitable material

◆ develop and print materials to support a presentation.

References

A Statement on English for Australian Schools. Curriculum Corporation, Melbourne, 1994.

Bloom, B (1956) *Taxonomy of Educational Objectives: The Classification of Educational Goals*. Longmans, London.

Davies, A et al. (1994) *Together Is Better: Collaborative Assessment, Evaluation and Reporting*. Eleanor Curtain, Melbourne.

De Bono, E (1988) *Six Thinking Hats*. In *Masterthinker 11* (kit). International Center for Creative Thinking, New York.

English: A Curriculum Profile for Australian Schools. Curriculum Corporation, Melbourne, 1994.

Freebody, P & Luke, A (1990) '"Literacies" Programs: Debate and Demands in Cultural Context'. *Prospect* Vol. 5, No. 3.

Wiederhold, C with Kagan, S (1995) *Cooperative Learning and Higher Level Thinking: The Q-matrix*. Kagan Cooperative Learning, San Juan Capistrano, California.

Chapter 2: Concepts and principles

The theory behind any program is what informs and drives it. Like most practitioners, I have been influenced by many theories and concepts over the years — too many to articulate here. I include the following because they are the most relevant in informing my present planning and teaching.

My teaching of reading over the last ten years has been supported by a growing understanding of the different aspects involved in becoming a successful reader. As my understanding has grown, so has my repertoire of strategies aimed at teaching those different aspects. It was Garth Boomer — one of the instigators of the national curriculum framework that resulted in the statement and profiles — who challenged me to make absolutely clear to myself, as a teacher, what I was requiring of my students. One of the ways I have set out to achieve this is to make my assessment criteria clear for my students.

The four roles of a reader, articulated by Freebody and Luke (1990), offered a framework that helped me to analyse the different aspects of reading I needed to include in my program. This analysis enabled me to identify the broad aims that I should set for my young readers. It also enabled me to identify outcomes that emerge from positioning students in each of these roles. Once this was clear in *my* head, I was able to make explicit to the students the criteria that they were to apply to their reading — and which, together, we would use to assess their achievements.

Four thinking and questioning frameworks have been notable in providing me with the organisational models necessary to clarify how students might pursue identified outcomes. These are the work of: De Bono (1988), who developed a 'six-hat' approach to thinking; Bloom (1956), who developed an organisational hierarchy of analytical skills; Wiederhold (1995), who devised a matrix encompassing a variety of thinking approaches; and O'Brien (1994) and Comber (1995), who developed a framework of questions and strategies for critical literacy in the classroom. The structure of the national English statement and profile also helped to tease out the various aspects I needed to address in my planning, teaching and assessment.

The need to tease out the elements of the learning that I wanted for my students fed inevitably into the assessment process — and into students' involvement in that process. I concluded that if students were to engage fully in their learning, they would need to have greater control of the assessment process; they would need to be involved in setting the criteria by which they would be judged, and in making their own judgements about the level of their achievements.

In what follows, then, I will briefly consider some of the concepts and principles that underpin my teaching of reading:

◆ explicit teaching

◆ four roles of the reader

◆ thinking and questioning approaches:

    – De Bono's six hats

    – Bloom's questioning model

    – Wiederhold's question matrix

    – critical literacy approaches

◆ authentic assessment.

Explicit teaching

Freebody, Ludwig and Gunn's notion of 'interactive trouble' (1995) has helped me to acknowledge how often teachers, myself included, create problems for students. Their work, summarised in what follows, has further convinced me that it is essential for the teacher to communicate explicitly in the classroom.

Interactive trouble

Peter Freebody and his colleagues (1995) have labelled the communication difficulties between student and teacher as 'interactive trouble'. All teachers have experienced difficulty in communicating ideas to another person, especially to the divergent thinker, or to the student who has misinterpreted a point that is basic to the understanding being developed. Teachers often work to elicit what they see as the 'correct' answer from a student group. Often, it is at this point that interactive trouble becomes obvious.

How often have you been surprised when your explanations have been met with blank faces or answers that are 'off track'? When this interactive trouble is considered, the word 'explicit' takes on a different meaning, and its importance becomes startlingly obvious.

Freebody has identified six different types of interactive trouble, which are discussed in what follows.

Epistemological trouble

Most questions rely upon shared knowledge and a shared context of understanding between the questioner and the answerer. That is why friends of long standing are able to converse in a 'shorthand' that is easily understood by both. Students are bound to experience difficulty whenever a teacher assumes that they have knowledge they in fact lack, or assumes that they know the type of answer sought when in fact they do not. Students who do not share the same culture or context as the teacher are those most likely to experience difficulties in this regard.

Organisational trouble

When a teacher wants to organise, say, a concept map, some student responses need to be 'put aside' so that the teacher's aim can be achieved. This presents particular problems to the teacher in organising and structuring the interaction. It presents even more trouble for the student seeking to determine what level of answer the teacher prefers. Thus, part of what students learn is that a correct answer is only correct if it is placed in the right 'slot' in the discussion as structured by the teacher.

Reasoning trouble

If we accept the view that all answers contributed by students are offered in good faith and have some reasoning to them, then wrong answers present particularly interesting sources of information for teachers. They can be a window into the student's reception and processing of information.

The reasoning used by students to produce apparently wrong answers often relies on the kind of logic that might be highly valued in another circumstance or in another place.

Pedagogical trouble

Often, a teacher holds a particular theory and the student provides an answer which is based on a different theory. Students need to be 'cued into' what the teacher is focusing on in the lesson. For example, a student may look at a whole word while the teacher is focusing on the individual sounds of the letters. It is through the teacher's explanation and questioning that students must infer the particular theory held by the teacher.

Relational trouble

Teachers often ask questions to which they already know the answers. However, they also ask questions to which they do not know the answers. The student must sort this distinction out for each question.

At other times, teachers require the student to discriminate between fantasy and reality, and then to operate within the chosen paradigm; similarly, the student may need to work out whether a teacher is inviting humour, play and speculation, or wants serious realism.

Stylistic trouble

Because of their occupational culture, teachers choose words and sentence structures with which students are not always familiar. This creates a style of speech that the student must decipher before understanding can be reached. To avoid this type of trouble, teachers must be aware of the different cultures that students bring with them to school, even those within the group that has English as a first language.

The practice of explicit teaching

The types of interactive trouble described above are inevitable in all classrooms. However, it is the teacher's role to be aware of points at which interactive trouble may occur, and to make clear the intentions, meanings and requirements that will support learning.

Explicit teaching is about giving students all the information needed for their learning. It requires the teacher to make clear the expectations, processes and specific outcomes of the learning.

The practice of being unambiguous and transparent about literacy learning is supported by many theorists. They include: Paris, Wixson and Palincsar (1986), who are concerned with developing independent, strategic readers; Westwood (1995), who advocates breaking learning into small, carefully taught steps; Derewianka (1990), who promotes a 'genre approach' to writing; as well as Freebody, Ludwig and Gunn (1995), whose work clearly suggests the need for demystifying literacy processes and purposes.

Very often, students are left guessing about how to become successful readers and writers. Sometimes this is because teachers are not clear about what students should do to learn these skills. Sometimes it is because teachers do not see the need to explain purposes, processes and outcomes because they assume that this is the domain of the professional.

The resulting confusion and ambiguity underlines Freebody, Ludwig and Gunn's description 'interactive trouble'. It is a teacher's responsibility to reduce confusion about literacy learning by looking closely at the processes of teaching and learning, so that teaching can be delivered in a way that is clear, focusing on the achievement of identified outcomes. As explained above, the assessment program is integral to making the learning explicit to the students.

Advantages of explicit programming

Being explicit in programming allows the teacher to have a clear 'head set' about the outcomes to be achieved and the structure that will be used to do so. Only with clear programming will the teacher have a sharp mental picture of the process that will be followed — and that is the first condition to be met if a teacher is to inform and instruct students explicitly. This will minimise interactive trouble, supporting students by providing a clear understanding of what is expected of them.

Without a doubt, it is important to use students' interests to build a stimulating program. However, a note of caution: this needs to be negotiated at the beginning; the cumulative value of this program will be greatly impaired if students are led off on a tangent whenever some artefact or idea arrives in the classroom. The program I will describe in this book achieves its teaching goals because the planning is extended across a year, enabling the gradual development of students' negotiation and management skills. You will observe that negotiation phases are built into the program; these are vital, and should not be overlooked.

Using outcomes to be explicit

The national English statement and profile provide clear and comprehensive outcomes for students and teachers to work towards. An explicit teaching program hinges on the selection of realistic outcomes that are appropriate to students' needs and level, and to the class setting and dynamics. Therefore, it is essential first to identify students' needs, then to select relevant, applicable outcomes, and then to choose resources before the program begins. From this, a clear pathway for teaching emerges, enabling the teacher to avoid interactive trouble and to guide students, in a structured way, towards the identified outcomes.

My knowledge of the national English statement and profile provides the continuum of learning from which the outcomes in my program are selected to meet the specific needs of the student group. I have identified the targeted outcomes in the 'Planning' section of each term's work (chapters 3–6).

I make a point of expressing outcomes according to purpose and audience. In the classroom, I first explain the intended outcomes to the class group, then post the whole set on the wall as a reference. I provide a similar set on the reporting sheet for parents that is included in the portfolios that are sent home. I only specify the relevant levels from the national curriculum profile for the purposes of school and state-based assessment. Most of the outcomes are from level 4; some aim to accommodate level 3, while others extend some students into level 5.

Four roles of the reader

Peter Freebody and Allan Luke (1990) have proposed that a successful reader in our society needs to be proficient in four different aspects. These are now referred to as the 'four roles of the reader'. It is useful to consider each role when planning and teaching a reading program.

Code breaker: How do I crack this?

In the role of code breaker, readers recognise and use sounds in words, spelling and structural conventions, and patterns — such as the grammar of the language — to break the written code. This enables them to interpret words, sentences, paragraphs and whole texts.

Text participant: What does this mean?

In this role, readers actively construct meaning from the text and pictures. To do this, they must draw on their own prior knowledge about life, school, the subject matter and other texts to infer a personal meaning from the text they are reading. Teachers need to encourage students to value their prior knowledge — to make links with previous experiences and to draw from what they already know as a basis for making meaning and extending their reading experiences.

Text user: What do I do with this here and now?

Readers become aware of the various types of text that apply to different audiences and situations. In this role, readers develop knowledge about where and when to use a variety of texts, both at school and in the wider community. The tone, formality and sequencing of texts are important aspects of this role.

Text analyst: What does all this do to me?

In this role, readers become aware that texts are constructed according to the views and interests of the author. Readers recognise that texts are not neutral, but express particular views that can be challenged. They recognise that texts may present a selective grouping of facts in which some views predominate and others are marginalised, or a perspective among many possible perspectives; equally, texts may hide or reveal their author. Students also need to realise that text places readers in particular stances — stances that may be challenged in a way that opens up other viewpoints.

It is vital to take each of these roles into account when setting up a reading program. All readers should be able to:

◆ decode and interpret texts

◆ make connections with the meaning of texts

◆ recognise and use different texts for their own intended purposes

◆ interrogate texts, and resist the impact of texts on their views and understandings of the world.

By checking my program against the four roles, I am able to ensure that each role is engaged.

Thinking and questioning approaches

De Bono's six hats

Edward De Bono (1988) has developed a model of thinking that encourages students to approach a problem from different entry points. To assist in this, problem solvers 'wear' different-coloured hats, each one suggesting the viewpoint that they are to adopt.

The six hats

Colour	Domain	Approach
Red	Feelings	Students describe how they feel about something.
Yellow	Strengths	Students consider what is good about something.
Black	Weaknesses	Students identify potential problems or difficulties.
Green	Ideas	Students consider what is possible; what else this might lead to.
White	Information	Students access and verify the truth about something.
Blue	Thinking	Students consider what thinking is needed to understand or move forward.

Note: Some teachers prefer to substitute purple for black to avoid negative associations with the colour black.

Bloom's questioning model

Benjamin Bloom's model (1956) describes six levels of thinking, sequentially arranged. It can be adapted for use in the classroom to encourage a broad range of thinking and questioning by students. The following explanations show how the six layers of thinking can be applied to pose questions about texts. Answers to these questions lead readers more deeply into texts; they also provide teachers with material for assessment of students' understanding.

◆ *Knowledge.* Students set questions that require recall of what has happened in the story they are studying.

◆ *Comprehension.* Students set questions requiring them to say what they know, in their own words. That is, the questions ask them to demonstrate understanding of the text's content.

◆ *Application.* Students set questions requiring them to take their learning from a text and apply it to other contexts.

◆ *Analysis.* Students set questions asking them to show that they understand the different parts of the text, and the contribution these parts make to the whole.

◆ *Evaluation.* Students set questions that ask them to give their own opinion about their reading, and to back this up with reasons.

◆ *Synthesis.* Students ask questions requiring them to develop an original thought or product built on knowledge and understanding gained from the text. When they take ideas or issues raised in a text and then present a different viewpoint, students are engaging in synthesis.

Bloom's model describes a hierarchical sequence. The lower levels, such as knowledge and comprehension, require more literal thinking, while the higher levels, such as evaluation and synthesis, require the student to think in a more complex manner.

Wiederhold's question matrix

Wiederhold (1995) devised a matrix (see opposite) that poses two dimensions of questions that can be applied to the reading of story texts. These lead students to investigate the elements of the texts — characters, events, situations etc — by asking questions about the present and past, then projecting into the future and considering these elements in new and creative ways. Like Bloom's taxonomy, the matrix encourages students to first ascertain what happened in the story, then to think creatively about it.

Present	What is?	Where/When is?	Which is?	Who is?	Why is?	How is?
Past	What did?	Where/When did?	Which did?	Who did?	Why did?	How did?
Possibility	What can?	Where/When can?	Which can?	Who can?	Why can?	How can?
Probability	What would?	Where/When would?	Which would?	Who would?	Why would?	How would?
Prediction	What will?	Where/When will?	Which will?	Who will?	Why will?	How will?
Imagination	What might?	Where/When might?	Which might?	Who might?	Why might?	How might?
	Event	Situation	Choice	Person	Reason	Means

Note that I have applied the matrix in term 3 (see p 73) in order to scaffold students' investigations in two key ways:

◆ as a means of enabling *coverage*, prompting students to extend their inquiry into, through and 'out of' the story

◆ to facilitate a *depth* of inquiry, challenging students to move below the level of what/where/when into analysis of how/why.

Critical literacy approaches

'Critical literacy' describes an approach to texts that encourages exploration of authors' biases and points of view. The approach assumes that readers need to understand the ways in which writers shape and manipulate their audience. Equipped with this understanding, readers can thus make their own judgements and form their own opinions. Both Hilary Janks (1993) and Jennifer O'Brien (1994) have described useful ways for teachers to enable students to question texts and form their own points of view. O'Brien's main work has been in lower primary, while Janks has worked mainly with secondary and tertiary students. However, their ideas can be adapted to empower younger readers.

In my classroom I have focused on students exploring:

◆ the orientations of the author

◆ the intended audience and purpose of the text

◆ who is represented and who is missing from the text

◆ whose point of view is taken in the text.

This is done through whole-class discussion, small-group work and reflective writing (see, for example, pp 114–118).

There is another aspect of critical literacy that informs my teaching, and that is the inevitability that my own values and perspectives will influence what and how I teach. My interpretation of text will also be coloured by my experiences and values. I acknowledge this in the classroom. I explain and demonstrate that my view is only one view, and that other views must be heard and valued.

An Explicit Reading Program

Authentic assessment

Assessment is a necessary part of the growth process, and should feel like it. I am committed to involving students in the assessment process, so that they have a sense of control in setting personal goals and planning their next steps. Thus, assessment becomes a natural part of learning, and students appreciate that it is not a system set up to trap them, but one which supports them to move on to greater successes. The criteria need to be clear, well explained and outlined up front, so that the target is fully understood by all.

'Authentic assessment' is assessment that is relevant to the student, informing him or her about successful demonstration of the component that is being learned or developed. It acknowledges a continuum of learning, encouraging learners to plot their present location and aim for further movement along that continuum.

Authentic assessment is used throughout the learning process. It is not a test designed to uncover students' recall at the end of a unit of teacher-delivered facts. Students are aware of the criteria for assessment; in many cases, this is negotiated at the beginning of the unit. The program in this book sets out to make clear to students the place of assessment in their learning, along with the criteria that will be applied to show their acquisition of knowledge and skills, and their movement along the continuum.

The forms of assessment used in this program are assignments, presentations, observations, portfolios and reflective writing. These are the same as those proposed by Parry and Gregory (1998) (who refer to them as projects, performances, observations, portfolios, learning logs and journals). The tools for assessment are drawn from a range of sources. They include: adaptations of Bloom's taxonomy; the Wiederhold question matrix; a criteria rubric and a criteria list with provision for comments by students, parents and teachers; a peer comment sheet; and structured reflection sheets.

Accountability is an important issue for assessment. If teachers are to be accountable to parents, and to education departments or districts — not to mention the society in general — for the progress and development of children, then outcomes must be articulated explicitly. We must be able to give accurate indications as to where students sit along the learning continuum. Not only will we meet the legitimate expectations of parents, bureaucracies and other interested parties, we will inform our own teaching, and meet the needs of students as they map their own pathways of learning. As outlined in chapter 1, communicating with parents is an integral part of this program, with letters and portfolios being the major mechanisms by which parents are informed of assessment tasks and criteria, and of their child's progress in relation to these.

Making a decision about the expectations and standards to be achieved from a unit of work is the first step in designing outcomes-based assessment. It must be clear to both teacher and student what will be valued, what the task will be, and what students are expected to know. Once decisions are made about the outcomes, learning experiences can be designed.

In this book, assignments are used as both the task *and* the assessment, thus providing an authentic assessment task with explicit requirements and negotiated content. Students are made familiar with the assessment sheets they will use as they develop their work in relation to the outcomes required. Assessment is ongoing and develops throughout the year, giving students a method by which they can locate themselves on the learning continuum and providing a developing picture of attainment for parents.

The program of assessment develops through the year. Students build their understanding of its components, steadily learning to take control as they become familiar with the process and the significance of the criteria. In term 1, the students receive an explicit explanation of the assignment and the related criteria — which, at this stage, are set by the teacher. In term 2, the assignment is again set by the teacher, but this time the criteria for achievement are negotiated. By term 3, students are using a framework which scaffolds them in designing their own assignment questions and criteria. Finally, in term 4, the students are in a position to use the elements and criteria they have learnt through the year to reflect knowledgeably on their own work.

Throughout this year, we have done three Reading Assignments, one each term except term four. I enjoyed all of them, but my favourite would have to be term 3's assignment. We had to study one book in depth and I chose "Looking for Alibrandi". We got to choose what we wanted to include in the assignment and there were many

aspects to it. Some of my favourite ones that I included were poetry, letter writing, designing, presentation and of course a speech at the end in front of the class. I thoroughly enjoyed working on the assignments and as a result, I received an A+.

Shanah

Shanah's end-of-program reflection on her attainments in reading and related competencies.

References

Bloom, B (1956) *Taxonomy of Educational Objectives: The Classification of Educational Goals.* Longmans, London.

De Bono, E (1988) *Six Thinking Hats.* In *Masterthinker 11* (kit). International Center for Creative Thinking, New York.

Derewianka, B (1990) *Exploring How Texts Work.* Primary English Teaching Association, Sydney.

English: A Curriculum Profile for Australian Schools. Curriculum Corporation, Melbourne, 1994.

Freebody, P, Ludwig, C & Gunn, S (1995) *Everyday Literacy Practices in and out of Schools in Low Socio-economic Urban Communities.* Curriculum Corporation, Melbourne.

Freebody, P & Luke, A (1990) '"Literacies" Programs: Debate and Demands in Cultural Context'. *Prospect* Vol. 5, No. 3.

Janks, H (1993) *Language, Identity and Power.* Hodder & Stoughton in assoc. with Witwatersrand University Press, Johannesburg.

Muspratt, S, Freebody, P & Luke, A (eds) (1997) *Constructing Critical Literacies: Teaching and Learning Textual Practice.* Allen & Unwin, Sydney.

O'Brien, J (1991) *Reading and Writing Years R–3.* Education Department of South Australia, Adelaide.

O'Brien, J (1991) *Reading and Writing Years 4–7.* Education Department of South Australia, Adelaide.

Paris, S, Wixson, K & Palincsar, A (1986) 'Instructional Approaches to Reading Comprehension'. In E Roth Kops (ed.) *Review of Research in Education.* American Educational Research Association, Washington, DC.

Parry, T & Gregory, G (1988) *Designing Brain-compatible Learning.* Hawker Brownlow Education, Melbourne.

Westwood, P (1995) 'What Should We Be Teaching Explicitly to At-risk Beginning Readers and Writers?' In *Cornerstones*, modules 6 and 7. South Australian Department of Education and Children's Services, Adelaide.

Wiederhold, C with Kagan, S (1995) *Cooperative Learning and Higher Level Thinking: The Q-matrix.* Kagan Cooperative Learning, San Juan Capistrano, California.

term one

Chapter 3: Engaging students in wide reading

Planning

It is a priority of the year's reading program to develop students' love of reading. This love can be fostered by supporting students' ability to select books that they will enjoy, and their capacity to discuss those books with one another. This is the basis upon which they can develop a deeper knowledge and appreciation of literature.

Part of this deeper appreciation is a knowledge of how authors and illustrators create their texts — the choices they make about topics, characters, themes, settings and structure. This knowledge can then be incorporated into students' own writing, and the students' learning in reading and writing becomes interdependent.

Term 1 establishes the central place of reading for understanding, and of making the links between reading and writing. This term of reading assignments is planned to start when the students arrive at the beginning of the year, sometime in the first week. This gives students the maximum amount of time to complete their work.

I have found that students need to have a number of skills well developed before a negotiated assignment can be undertaken in term 3. To do this, I target:

◆ time management — students need careful teaching and support in prioritising and monitoring their work

◆ task management — students must monitor the progress, and evaluate the standard, of their work to achieve the intended outcomes

◆ book selection — the school library is used, as well as the expertise of the teacher librarian

◆ layout of book work — conventions and standards of organisation and presentation must be exemplified and understood.

While these are basic skills, it is essential that students have the opportunity to develop them over the term. I have designed this assignment with that development in mind. The skills are taught and supported so that students have a level of mastery that underlies their negotiated work in the following terms.

The specific skills that I teach explicitly in this assignment are chosen for their value in supporting reading, and to encourage a wide appreciation of books. I also link students' book investigations with the writing being undertaken in the classroom. For example, students look closely at the development of character in the stories they read during this term — a study that feeds into their own development of character when writing narrative.

Targeted outcomes

Students:

◆ read a wide variety of books at an appropriate reading level

◆ recognise the purposes of all publishing conventions in a book

◆ design, construct and use a database as a method of keeping records

◆ use prediction as a skill for choosing books and making meaning

◆ take notes and use them for writing up findings from non-fiction books

◆ use the research strategy of posing questions and locating answers

◆ are aware of the role of illustrations in picture books, how they are linked with text and how they are part of reading

◆ are aware of the ways in which authors develop authentic characters, and use this awareness in their writing

◆ develop their ability to visualise the scenes described in novels read

◆ are aware of all the information contained on the cover of a novel, where to find it and how to use it

◆ use correct punctuation when recording direct speech

◆ enjoy reading and participate in enjoyable activities associated with reading.

These outcomes are mostly situated in band B of the national statement on English (Reading and Viewing), with some drawn from band C. They encompass the broad outcomes in levels 3 and 4 of the national English profile (Reading and Viewing), and include some of the broad outcomes from level 5.

To achieve these outcomes with the students, I plan explicit lessons, then negotiate with the students the order in which they will be taught. This is the beginning of negotiation in the program. The order will be based on such factors as the availability of resources, students' interests and preferences, and the order in which students would like to tackle the assignment. I teach the following areas explicitly:

- The design and use of a database
- Questions and note-taking as a research strategy
- Pictures and social comment in picture books
- The writing and punctuation of direct speech
- Characterisation in story-writing.

Lesson outlines for each of these topics are included in this chapter, along with the continuous assessment pro forma for the term.

Some parts of the assignment are not taught explicitly. These are considered to contain skills and content that the students already have. They are included to give the students some sense of a starting point, and to reinforce the idea that students have prior knowledge upon which they can build further achievements. These activities remain valid and useful for the students' investigations, allowing them to launch from the known into the unknown.

Introducing the assignment

I introduce the assignment to the students by reading through with them the 'Term 1 reading assignment' sheet (see over). I then explain:

- the requirements of each activity
- which questions will be supported by teaching lessons, and that students must wait until these lessons start before commencing the related assignment activity
- that section 5 requires *each* activity to be completed — a different one for each book — but that students may select which activity to apply to each of their chosen books
- how work should be set out
- that time management needs to be considered and closely monitored. I suggest here that highlighting the activities as they are completed is a trick that will maintain students' focus and allow them to keep tabs on their progress. I also use a highlighter when marking each completed activity.

I explain the need for the explicit lessons — to introduce new concepts and ideas. We then discuss the order of the lessons. I suggest that the picture-book lessons be held first, as this will allow students to progress through the assignment with greater ease and speed. The rest of the order is then decided upon.

Term 1 reading assignment

This term you are required to read nine books:

- four novels (fiction)

- three picture books (fiction)

- two information books (non-fiction).

Make sure that you choose books suited to your reading level. For each book, complete the relevant activities. Then move on to a new book.

This assignment is to be presented neatly in your reading book. Make sure that the setting out is orderly, neat and clearly presented. Rule off each section as it is finished. Bring each section for assessment as soon as you finish it.

Activities

1. **All books**: Make a chart recording:

   - name of author, illustrator and publisher

   - publishing date

   - type of book

   - number of pages

   - how long it took you to read it

   - a short evaluation.

   Use these chart headings to construct a database on which to keep a record of all the books you read this year.

2. **Fiction books only**: Before you start to read the book, write a paragraph predicting what you think it will be about.

   Non-fiction books only: Before you start to read the book, write five questions to which you think you might find answers in this book.

3. **Information books only**: Take notes as you read the book, then use the notes to present an information page to display in the classroom. Place the notes in your reading book; place the information page on the wall.

4. **Picture books only**:

   - Explain how the pictures have been used to make the meaning of the text easier to understand.

   - State the age group for which you think the book has been written.

   - Explain what attracted you to choose this book, then evaluate it (say what you thought of it).

5. **Novels only**: Complete one of the following activities for each novel you have chosen. Do not repeat an activity.

- Choose a character, then complete a character web to develop ideas about her or him. Write a paragraph describing the qualities of the character. Explain why you would/wouldn't like to have this character as a friend.

- Make a mini diorama of a scene from the book. Make sure that you include a foreground and background. Clean up after using any paint. In your reading book, explain why you have chosen this particular scene, and say how it fits into the story.

- Make a new dust cover for your book. Remember to include all the relevant information, pictures and labels.

- Find some dialogue in the novel that records a conversation that explains something that has happened. Copy it into your reading book, making sure that you have copied the punctuation and spelling correctly.

This assignment is to be completed by the end of week 10. Because all the marking will be done as you complete the work for each book, there will be only one activity to mark in the final week.

Have a great term reading!

Communicating with parents

 When the assignment is given to the students, a letter is sent to parents, explaining the proposed reading program for the term.

Dear Parent,

This term the children have been given a reading assignment that asks them to read a number of books of varying types. Specifically, they are required to:

- *read nine books:*

    - *four novels*

    - *three picture books*

    - *two information books*

- *complete an activity for each book*

- *keep a record of the books read, both in table form and as a computer database.*

I will teach the students how to:

- *use pictures to help make meaning from text*

- *design and use a computer database*

- *take notes from information texts*

- *use questions as a research strategy*

- *write and punctuate direct speech*

- *develop characters in story-writing.*

Students will only attempt activities when the related teaching has been completed.

You can help at home by discussing the chosen books with your child. You may even wish to support your child's work by reading some of the books or helping to structure the management of the assignment. One skill I want to support and develop is time management. This can often present problems, and some experience in this area will stand students in good stead for high school and beyond.

If you have any questions about this program, or would like to join us for a lesson at any time, please let me know or make a time for discussion.

Regards

Kerry Gehling

Presentation requirements

Students are required to present their first term's assignment in their 'reading book' (an exercise book). The expectation is that their work will be neatly presented, ruled off and brought to the teacher for marking at the conclusion of each activity.

Students are also made aware that when they complete their progressive assessment sheet, it will form part of the portfolio sent home at the end of the unit. The content of this sheet, along with samples of completed sections, is provided at the end of this chapter.

Getting started

Having introduced students and parents to the term's assignment, I take the class to the library. Here, the teacher librarian and I work with the students to choose books for the study. I recommend that one of each type — novel, picture book, information book — is chosen to start.

During the early weeks of the term, reading lessons are taken up with explicit teaching lessons. Sustained silent reading (SSR) is a necessary daily component. I also set reading as homework two or three times per week.

Because students will be working on different sections of the assignment, I require them to nominate what they will do for homework, and to set themselves achievement goals for the night. They record these goals in their diaries. We also discuss achievement goals for the week. These are mapped on the board, and students known to require extra prompting are counselled. This keeps students aware of the time that they must manage, and provides them with a motivation to meet their own deadlines.

Explicit teaching

The design and use of a database

The students in my class are experienced computer users, having had regular lessons using computers since they began school. The class has a weekly, 45-minute lesson in the networked computer room, which has 30 units, so that each student is able to work alone. A large screen allows for teacher demonstrations.

I introduce databases knowing that all in the class have used the library database. However, despite the typical presence of a group of computer buffs, none has ordinarily had experience in creating a database at the point when I introduce this skill.

The major idea of this task is to design a re-usable database to record the required information for each book that students read. This concept is difficult for most students to grasp, so I use the idea of a box of recipe cards to illustrate it (and bring my recipe cards from home to illustrate the concept clearly).

Once students grasp that their design will be used for *each* book, they progress well, and are soon using personalised databases to record their reading. Typically, we use three lessons in the networked room to construct the databases and prepare one record. After that, the students enter progressive records of their reading in the classroom, where we have a single computer which is included in the network.

Lesson 1

This lesson teaches students to:

◆ design a re-usable template for a form

◆ use the forms once the template has been constructed.

Because the students are often at different points of learning in computing, it is important to ascertain, by questioning, what knowledge and skills are held in common and what must be explicitly demonstrated. The following questions help to steer the discussion. The answers consolidate the knowledge of some students while opening new understandings for others.

◆ What do you already know about databases?

◆ How are databases used by society? (Discussion prompts here might include the school library, hospitals, banks and shops.)

The use of our reading database is then explained. A database template is drawn on the board while relevant terms are being introduced. With students suggesting the field names needed, construction of the template begins. We use Microsoft Works for this purpose, but any software supporting database design may be used. Students are encouraged to personalise their own templates with colour and font choices.

Lesson 2

Construction continues, while terms and processes are revised. At this point, those students with a depth of computer experience become a valuable peer resource.

Lesson 3

Now with a working template, students enter data for as many books as they have read, printing off one record for inclusion in their portfolios.

Glossary of terms

Field	Part of a record that contains a particular category of information
Form	The display that shows each record
Record	The collection of information about a particular item, eg each book
Report	A print-out of database information, formatted and organised according to the user's specifications
Table	A listing of the information in records and fields, shown as rows for records and columns for fields
Template	A group of fields that are arranged at the beginning to set up the design of the form

Self-assessment

The resulting computer print-outs look very professional, and the students are always very pleased with them. Some students, however, achieve this outcome with a deal of support from their peers or the teacher. It is important that they have time to reflect on their own learning. To do this, students are required to fill out a 'Database self-assessment' pro forma (see over) in which they can acknowledge the help they have received and the level of skills that they have developed.

Useful words for filling out the reflection sheet are discussed in the class. Students may adapt these words if they feel constrained by any of those identified.

The self-assessment demonstrates that reflection and assessment are able to support learning. The students realise that honest reflection on their achievements allows them to identify where they are 'up to' in their learning. This is a basis from which they can determine what they still need to learn or practise. I encourage this awareness in all assessment tasks undertaken throughout the year. My aim is to develop the students' ability to reflect on their learning, to take control of seeking help, and to be proud of their achievements.

Database self-assessment

Task

Using Microsoft Works, create a database to record information about the books you have read this term. Enter information about each book. Be prepared to use the database to record information about all of the books you read through the year.

Outcome

Students feel confident in using Microsoft Works to create and maintain a database to use as a recording tool.

Self-assessment

1. I feel .... to create a database without help from anyone else.

2. In constructing the database, I gained the following knowledge and skills:

   ....

   ....

   ....

   ....

3. I would feel confident to teach someone else to create a database.   Yes / No

4. Other uses I could make of a database are:

   ....

   ....

   ....

   ....

Student comment:

Teacher comment:

Parent comment:

Questions and note-taking as a research strategy

 All students in the middle years will have had some experience with research and note-taking. However, few will have been taught the skills explicitly. My goal is that, after this topic, most students will be able to conduct their own research and take effective notes from the information that they locate. The lessons usually occur within a week, enabling the students to progress with their assignments.

Lesson 1: Questions

The class jointly considers a non-fiction big book; I usually use *The First Lunar Landing* (Martin, Badger & Comber, 1990). Together, we look at the cover and flip through the book to gain an impression of the topic.

Students are prompted to think of some questions that may be answered within the book. They may make such suggestions as:

◆ When did people first land on the moon?

◆ What are the names of the first people to walk on the moon?

At this point, I suggest that we might be able to draw a greater *depth* of information by asking more open-ended questions. We then work together to construct additonal open-ended questions. For example:

◆ Were there some criteria to be met by people who were chosen to be part of the first mission to the moon?

◆ What might have happened to the astronauts if something went wrong? What precautions were taken?

◆ What specialists were needed to mount the mission to the moon?

Together, we read through the book once. Answers are identified as we do so. If answers to any of the questions cannot be found, students are prompted to suggest where further information might be located.

Lessons 2 and 3: Note-taking

The First Lunar Landing is revisited. Students are asked to gather around the 'big book stand', and to bring note-taking equipment with them.

Each page is read through. Together, we decide what information might be important, then write notes. In this process, we pay attention to putting the points in our own words, not copying from the book. I usually promote this by the simple expediency of shutting the book. Dot points are used rather than sentences.

The terms 'topic sentences' and 'hyper theme' are introduced; we then discuss their usefulness in note-taking. We observe that the first sentence in a paragraph often contains the main point — a recognition that is useful in note-taking and skim reading.

Once the notes have been taken — and this sometimes takes more than one lesson — students form groups of two or three. These groups discuss their notes and, together, write up the four facts that they consider to be the most interesting or important. If necessary, groups refer back to the book. The class reconvenes and the reporter from each group reads that group's contribution.

Students are now equipped to complete the non-fiction section of the term's assignment, after which they record their response on the continuous assessment sheet.

Pictures and social comment in picture books

The work on picture books builds on the extensive experience the students have already had with this text type. The focus here is on considering the role of the pictures in each text, identifying the audience for which the book is intended, and expressing a personal response.

I also introduce the notion that there are significant *issues* in books. Because we read them together, picture books are ideal for introducing the complex ideas that books frequently embed. The identification of deeper issues in books is followed up in more detail as the year unfolds; by term 3, students are ready to locate these issues in their own reading.

The following four lessons fit into a week, each taking 40–60 minutes. The lessons draw out the ways in which pictures complement text in picture books. The resulting chart explicitly articulates the variety of ways that are identified. The issues identified for each selected book are used only as discussion points — a precursor to the issues that will be explored in more detail in the students' own choice of books later in the year. They are not taught explicitly here.

Lesson 1

The class discusses picture books and students consider the question: 'What is a picture book?'. Selected picture books are read to the class group, which jointly discusses the ways in which the pictures are used.

The following questions structure class discussion:

◆ In which ways do the pictures and the story go together?

◆ Do the pictures give more information when added to the text? In what way?

♦ How does the illustrator use colour?

♦ From whose point of view is the story told? Is this the same in the pictures?

♦ What issues are there in the book? How do the pictures deal with, or inform us about, these issues?

Any number of picture books could be selected for this discussion. I have used *Window* (Baker, 1991), *Crocodile Beat* (Jorgensen, 1989), *Just Another Ordinary Day* (Clements, 1995) and *Way Home* (Hathorn, 1994) with success. Each of these books uses pictures in a different way to expand on and support the text.

These books are used to begin a chart of the different ways that pictures are used in texts.

Lesson 2

This lesson provides a further opportunity to read books, identify how pictures are used and add to the charted features. I recommend *Luke's Way of Looking* (Wheatley, 1999), *The Visitors Who Came to Stay* (McAfee, 1984), *The Lost Thing* (Tan, 2000) and *The Watertower* (Crew, 1994) as starting points.

From the discussion, I continue the chart of points identifying the ways in which pictures are employed. I then post the completed chart in the classroom for reference in further lessons, and when students are completing the picture-book activities in their assignment.

Lesson 3

Each student is asked to select a picture book to bring to this lesson, making sure that it is one of sufficient depth or having particular interest in its visual content. Since they know that the library is open for borrowing before and after school, as well as during lunchtimes, students are expected to organise themselves.

A version of the 'think, pair, share' strategy is then used to discuss the selected books. With a partner, each student reads their choice of picture book, then explains how the pictures are used in conjunction with the text. Clear explanations must be given, with reference to the charted list.

Groups of two are then joined to make groups of four. These expanded groups select one of their books to report on to the class. The reporter, chosen by the group, shows the book and explains how the pictures are used with the text. The story is not read, but shown, explained and evaluated by way of recommendation or otherwise. These recommendations provide important support for students in selecting suitable texts for their term's assignment.

An Explicit Reading Program

Lesson 4

Partners write a letter to thank each other for the reading and to give feedback on the explanation and ideas provided. This is a form of assessment; I look for appropriateness in the form and tone of the letter, and relevant detail in the feedback. The letters are included in the students' portfolios.

At this point, students are free to complete the assignment activities about picture books (see p 26).

The writing and punctuation of direct speech

Explicit consolidation of the correct use of punctuation is valuable at any year level. Direct speech continues to cause difficulty even at the middle-school stage. Only one full lesson is required, but several additional ten-minute 'brain warmers' are suggested. These can be included across several terms, as needed.

Lesson 1

Students jointly view an overhead transparency displaying an extract that includes direct speech. The passage is read. Students' suggestions are used to highlight the actual words spoken. Then the punctuation marks around the speech are explained.

As they engage with the passage, the students identify the rules for punctuation of direct speech. These are made into a 'features list' to be posted in the classroom.

- Speech marks are placed around the ACTUAL words spoken.
- Punctuation — commas, full stops, question marks etc — is placed at the end of words spoken, INSIDE the speech marks.
- When the same person continues to speak, a new line is not necessary.
- When a new person speaks, a new line is started.
- When one person's speech has more than one paragraph, the speech marks still go only at the beginning and the end of the spoken words.

Students then form groups of four or five. The groups work with an extract, from an appropriate book, which has been chopped into sections like a jigsaw puzzle. A selection of punctuation marks is provided separately. Groups put the extract back together, positioning the punctuation in the correct places. Once all groups finish, they view the correct construction on the overhead projector.

The following example is taken from *Worry Warts* (Gleitzman, 1996). The sentences — and, in some cases, phrases — are typed on separate lines and boxed for ease of cutting out.

"We are not," thundered Dad, "going on holiday."

"But you've got to," pleaded Keith.

"Why have we?" asked Mum.

Keith took a breath. He had to say it.

"So you can stop talking about splitting up."

There was a long silence.

Mum and Dad exchanged a look.

Keith's insides felt like they were in a spin-drier.

Then Dad stepped forward and put his hands on Keith's shoulders and spoke slowly and softly.

"If you've heard us saying anything about splitting up, it's not what you think. We've been talking about splitting up in the shop, that's all."

There was another long silence.

We are not	thundered Dad
going on holiday	But you've got to
pleaded Keith	Why have we
asked Mum	Keith took a deep breath.

He had to say it.

So you can stop talking about splitting up

There was a long silence.

Mum and Dad exchanged a look.

Keith's insides felt like they were in a spin-drier.

Then Dad stepped forward and put his hands on

Keith's shoulders

and spoke slowly and softly

If you've heard us saying anything

about splitting up

it's not what you think

We've been talking about

splitting up in the shop

that's all

There was another long silence

"	"	"	"	"	"
"	"	"	"	"	"
?	,	,	,	,	,
.	.	.	.	.	.

At this point, students should be able to complete the assignment activity about speech (in activity 5, p 27). I suggest that students bookmark a suitable passage of dialogue when they see it, because it is always difficult to find just the right passage once it has been passed by. A stick-on note is suggested.

Lesson 2

Over several ten-minute sessions, students rewrite passages that contain speech but have had the punctuation marks omitted. These passages are displayed on the board. I correct the board version while the students check their own work. These sessions provide much-needed practice, reinforcing the ideas and rules that have been posted on the 'features list'. I often use this activity as an early-morning brain-warming session.

Characterisation in story-writing

Developing the qualities, rather than just the physical attributes, of a character is a difficult skill to master. Students need to be able to identify the techniques used by authors in the books they read if they are themselves to develop the characters about whom they are writing.

During term 1, the writing program in my classroom often contains some narrative writing. Horror or fantasy are usually chosen, as they are so often the genres that middle-years students choose to read.

Writing by expert authors is chosen to model the way characters are developed by describing emotions, motives, reactions and speech. Passages suitable for these lessons are difficult to find, and I am constantly on the lookout for them. Good starting points are:

◆ *45 and 47 Stella Street: And Everything that Happened* (Elizabeth Honey)

◆ *Windmill at Magpie Creek* (Christobel Mattingley)

◆ *Jodie's Journey* (Colin Thiele).

Students follow an extract that is read out; I then model a character web (see p 41) to show how character qualities can be recorded. The following examples are taken from *45 and 47 Stella Street: And Everything that Happened*.

When Rob and Donna get home they are MORTIFIED when they hear what happened. Straight away they go and knock on the Phonies' door and apologise. Frank, the little knucklehead, thinking that it might soften them up a bit says

"Briquette is sick."

"The little guts deserves to die," says Mrs Phonie.

"Painfully," says Mr Phonie, and slams the door.

Source: Honey, E (1995) 45 & 47 Stella Street: And Everything that Happened. Allen & Unwin, Sydney.

There were more calls to Mr Smeeton. Donna never lost her temper. That's probably how she got the job she has. She never loses her temper. Rob would have told the Phonies to take a long walk off a short pier. Mum would have gone quiet. She just buttons up. Dad would have lost his temper, for sure, and called them inconsiderate pea brains. But not Donna. She just keeps on keeping on.

Eventually it was decided the height of the fence would remain the same.

Donna sure got to know Mr Smeeton on the phone. Although he didn't say it, she could tell Mr Smeeton was getting fed up with the Phonies too.

Ever-patient Donna cleared away her garden that was beside the fence, lugging all the pots and containers round the back. She wanted to get it over with before the spring. At last there was nothing left beside the fence but the Apricot tree and a couple of bushes. It looked as if everything else had fled before the battle.

Source: Ibid.

Here, Donna is portrayed as being patient and kind; in contrast, the neighbours — 'the Phonies' — are unpleasant and cruel. The language and incidents that indicate these qualities are jointly identified through discussion; as this occurs, the teacher can model the completion of a character web.

The following questions could provide focus for this discussion:

◆ What does this character do that shows his or her personality?

◆ Does the character speak in a way that illustrates something about her/his personality?

◆ What type of adjectives or descriptive phrases does the author use to describe this character's personality?

As part of this term's assignment, the students are required to complete a character web (see opposite) for one of the novels they read, and to use this as a graphic organiser for a piece of writing about that character. This analysis will increase in depth in term 3, where characters' emotions and motives are explored, and the students' understandings of them are assessed.

Character web

1. Select two characters from the novel you have chosen.

2. List six words that describe each character.

Character 1	Character 2
....	....
....	....
....	....
....	....
....	....
....	....

3. Complete a character web for one of these characters. Write his or her name in the centre of the web. Along each spoke of the web, write a word that describes the qualities of your chosen character.

4. Think of an incident in the story that demonstrates each quality. Write this in the oval at the end of each spoke.

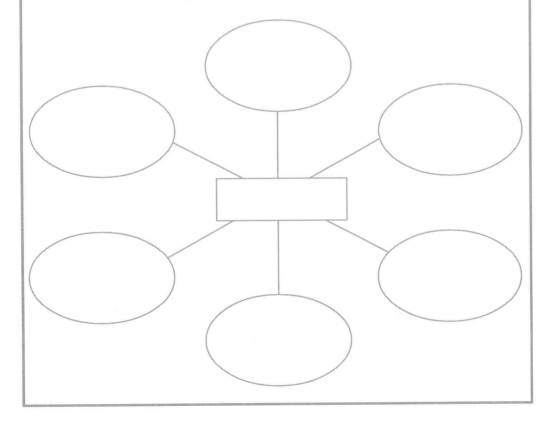

Assessment

An assessment sheet is used both to record progress and assess work. As students complete each activity in their reading book, they bring me the book and assessment sheet; I check this off and write a comment about the quality of the work presented. Generally, I simply tick off the activity itself in the book, although I recommend that comments be placed here if alterations are necessary. I make most comments on the assessment sheet.

At the end of the term, when the last assignment activity has been marked and commented upon, a summative teacher comment relating to the whole assignment can be added in the box provided. Each student can then add a self-assessment before taking the sheet home for parent comment.

Reading assessment, term 1

Targeted outcomes

Students:

- read a wide variety of books at an appropriate reading level

- recognise the purposes of all publishing conventions in a book

- design, construct and use a database as a method of keeping records

- use prediction as a skill for choosing books and making plans

- take notes and use them for writing up findings from non-fiction books

- use the research strategy of posing questions and locating answers

- are aware of the role of illustrations in picture books, how they are linked with text and how they are part of reading

- are aware of the ways in which authors develop authentic characters, and use this awareness in their writing

- develop their ability to visualise the scenes described in novels read

- are aware of all the information contained on the cover of a novel, where to find it and how to use it

- use correct punctuation when recording direct speech

- enjoy reading and participate in enjoyable activities associated with reading.

Record the books as you read them this term.

Novels

1. ....
2. ....
3. ....
4. ....

Picture books

1. ....
2. ....
3. ....

Information books

1. ....
2. ....

Chart completed, including all relevant information   [   ]

Database completed   [   ]

Predictions

1. ....
2. ....
3. ....
4. ....
5. ....
6. ....
7. ....

Investigation questions

1. ....
2. ....

Activities

1. Poster

2. Poster

3. Picture book (a)

4. Picture book (b)

5. Picture book (c)

6. Novels

Activity 1

Activity 2

Activity 3

Activity 4

Time management

....

....

....

Teacher comment:

Student comment:

Parent comment:

Activities
1. Poster

Some interesting info Jack. Remember to do some proof reading before you bring it for marking.

2. Poster

Very interesting information - I learnt something new.

3. Picture books

(a) Well explained

Excellent Jack. you obviously thought well about this book with no words.

[C] Constructive observations & comments.

Above and over: Samples from Jack's term 1 assessment sheet.

4. Novels

Activity 1.
Attractive and eye-catching dust cover.
All necessary information included (e.g.
title, author, spine etc) No. 13/3

Activity 2.
I like the interaction you have chosen. It really
shows how the parent and child are
relating.

Student comment
Reading Assingment was a great challenge
which I really enjoyed. I'm very glad
I finished early which allowed time
for other projects. I chose the right
books for reading. I liked the setup too.

Parent comment Great idea a variety of
books certainly keep the
kids entertained well done

References

Baker, J (1991) *Window*. Julia MacRae, London.

Clement, R (1995) *Just Another Ordinary Day*. Angus & Robertson, Sydney.

Crew, G (1994) *The Watertower*. Era Publications, SA.

Gleitzman, M (1996) *Worry Warts*. Pan, Sydney.

Hathorn, L (1994) *Way Home*. Random House, Sydney.

Honey, E (1995) *45 & 47 Stella Street: And Everything that Happened*. Allen & Unwin, Sydney.

Jorgensen, G (1989) *Crocodile Beat*. Omnibus Books, Adelaide.

Martin, R, Badger, L & Comber, B (eds) (1990) *The First Lunar Landing*. Big book. Era Publications, SA.

Mattingley, C (1971) *Windmill at Magpie Creek*. Hodder & Stoughton, Sydney.

McAfee, A & Browne, A (1984) *The Visitors Who Came to Stay*. Hamish Hamilton, London.

Tan, S (2000) *The Lost Thing*. Lothian Books, Melbourne.

Wheatley, N (1999) *Luke's Way of Looking*. Hodder Headline Australia, Sydney.

Chapter 4: A closer look at authors

Planning

In term 1, the program established the centrality of wide reading for understanding, along with a 'reading culture' in the classroom. It also set up the links between reading and writing, and the importance of personal time management. In term 2, a focus remains on broad reading, but selection of material occurs within specified parameters. The aim in this term is to raise students' awareness of authors' styles and strategies.

Any parameters could be set in order to engage the whole class in cooperative work, in which students share their findings and learnings. I have confined students' book selection to Australian authors. I have done so for several reasons:

◆ I believe it is important to know the authors and texts that inform students about their own heritage and experiences, whether these have been lifelong or recent.

◆ Elements of texts set in a familiar context are easier for students to understand.

◆ Books by Australian authors are readily available. We can access many titles — novels, picture books and information texts.

It is also possible to make links from the English program to Studies of Society and Environment. One of my classes developed, during this second term, a brochure about a part of Australia. To do this, the students needed to explore and describe in persuasive text.

While my students are by now familiar with the process of reading assignments, this term's assignment hones their skills and develops new skills. Time management is once again an issue. It is discussed in detail, and is often a topic for the three-way conference held in the middle of the year. As in term 1, I keep a time management chart in a prominent location, we set weekly goals of achievement, and the diary is used for setting homework goals and keeping parents informed.

Targeted outcomes

The outcomes targeted in this assignment extend those of the previous term. Students:

◆ continue reading a wide variety of books

◆ use the database constructed in term 1

◆ develop knowledge of characterisation, with further attention to the development of a character's emotions

◆ develop knowledge of setting and investigate authors' use of adjectives to make settings vivid

◆ develop a knowledge of Australian authors through exposure to their work

◆ investigate one Australian author

◆ identify pointers that indicate that writing is Australian

◆ identify the characteristics of a book review, and write a book review.

These outcomes build towards the attainment of reading outcomes in band B of the national curriculum profile. In some cases, students will achieve outcomes in band C. To support these outcomes, I provide explicit teaching throughout the assignment in the following areas:

◆ Writing a book review

◆ Investigating characters' emotions

◆ Australian writing

◆ Development of setting

◆ Types of books.

Lesson outlines for each of these areas are included in this chapter. The order of the teaching lessons follows the order presented to students in 'Term 2 reading assignment' (see opposite). The students work on the author study for a week before I introduce them to the rubric that is the basis for the assessment of their study.

Introducing the assignment

I introduce the assignment in the first week of term 2. Together, we work through 'Term 2 reading assignment' (see following). Again, I make clear:

◆ what is required in each activity

◆ which questions will be supported by teaching lessons, and will therefore need to be attempted after this support is given

◆ what is expected in the presentation of work

◆ that students will need to manage their own time, drawing on their experience with this skill in term 1.

Term 2 reading assignment

This term, you are required to choose books by Australian authors. You must read the works of at least two authors, and you must read at least two works by each author.

Your selection must include:

• four novels

• two picture books

• two information books.

Activities

1. **Author study**: Find out as much as you can about one of your chosen authors. Include the following information:
   • A list of books written by the author
   • The type of book this author writes
   • A review of your favourite book by this author
   • Some personal details about the author
   • Any other interesting facts that you discover in your investigation.

2. **Character study**: Choose one character from the books you have read this term. Use a character web to introduce this character to other readers.

3. **Characters' emotions**: Explain how one author has written about the emotions of the characters in his or her book. Include:
   • the kind of emotions the characters show
   • the ways in which the author develops these emotions
   • a passage in which the author uses words skilfully to reveal feelings.

4. **Descriptive writing**: From the books you have selected, find a description that really appeals to you. Explain why it is appealing. What has the author done to make it really live for you?

---

5. **Australian writing**: You have chosen Australian authors. In their books, what shows that the authors are Australian? Is it the way they write, the settings they use, the doings of the characters, or maybe something else?

    Consider one of your selected books. Explain what it is about the book that tells you that it was written by an Australian. Perhaps you do not feel that the book contains anything that demonstrates this. If so, explain.

Communicating with parents

 At the beginning of the term, I prepare an explanatory letter to parents, recapping the previous term's work and explaining the term ahead. This is sent home when the assignment is given out.

Dear Parent,

Last term's reading assignment was most successful. Students showed great interest in the picture books for older readers, and were able to develop their knowledge of the use of pictures in these books. I am impressed with the learning achieved about databases and the uses that students are now making of their note-taking skills.

This term we will undertake an assignment that investigates an Australian author in depth. I will teach the students about:

- *writing a book review*
- *investigating characters' emotions*
- *Australian writing*
- *development of setting*
- *types of books.*

The biggest problem that the students encountered last term was in managing their time. I will support this aspect at school by keeping a priority listing on the board; I will also send home diary notes to keep you informed. Your help in discussing these matters would be a great support for your child.

The students and I will negotiate the term's outcomes next week. When that is done, we will construct a rubric — a scale describing different levels of performance that the students might demonstrate as they work to achieve each outcome. I will post this rubric in the classroom for students to refer to. At the end of the term, your child's work will be assessed using this rubric, which will be sent home in the portfolio. Look out, too, for other assessment sheets as we finish some of the teaching sessions.

Thank you for your continued support.

Regards

Kerry Gehling

Presentation requirements

Students are required to present their author study in a poster format; they present other parts of the assignment in their reading books. The expectations of organisation and clarity are the same as for term 1, and students should be conversant with them. An assessment sheet — this time in the form of a rubric — forms part of each student's portfolio, and is sent home at the end of the unit.

Negotiation of rubric

A tool that I find valuable for assessment — and as a target for student achievement — is a rubric. A rubric consists of a fixed scale annotated with a set of characteristics describing what performance should look like at each point on the scale. Rubrics have two major advantages: they describe expectations that are clear to teachers and parents; and they provide students with a clear target.

Rubrics are usually presented to students at the same time as the task is assigned. However, I negotiate the outcome levels with my students in week 2, allowing them a week to consider the assignment.

On a large piece of paper, I list the tasks to be performed. Then, together, we negotiate what the student outcomes might look like — that is, we decide what a response would look and sound like if it were to achieve a high rating or score. The same process is followed for low and medium scores. Having had the assignment sheet for about a week, the students have a picture of the types of responses necessary. However, they may not have thought this through thoroughly. Speaking and negotiating together makes all in the class very well aware of the performance expectations as they are discussed, dissected and decided upon cooperatively.

Once all the sections of the rubric have been decided upon, a large copy is posted in the classroom. When my students use rubrics, I often see them consulting the required outcomes as they move through the assignment. In fact, I insist that they consult it before they hand in the completed assignment.

The following page spreads provide:

◆ a template of the rubric used

◆ an example of the outcomes negotiated with one of my classes.

Name: ....

	Low	Medium	High
1. Author study			
List the books written by this author.			
Review a book by this author.			
Identify the type of book this author writes.			
Locate and provide personal details about the author.			
Provide other interesting information or illustrations.			
2. Character study			
Complete a character web.			

Name: ....

Activity	Low	Medium	High
3. Characters' emotions			
What emotions do the characters show?			
How does the author develop these emotions or feelings?			
Find a passage in which the author uses words skilfully to develop feelings.			
4. Choice of descriptive passage			
Choose a book passage (half a page or more).			
What strategies has the author used to make this description come alive for you?			
5. What does the author do in the books that shows she/he is Australian?			
6. Presentation			
Present your study in poster form, and in your reading book.			

Name: ....

Activity	Low	Medium	High
1. Author study			
List the books written by this author.	List attempted	Incomplete list	Complete list or partial with explanation
Review a book by this author.	Story title given Recount given Opinion offered	Story title given A little about the author Plot and setting described Characterisation described Opinion given	Excellent review construction Title of story Descriptions discussed Detail about the author Plot and setting commented upon Characterisation discussed Opinion given
Identify the type of book this author writes.	Showing lack of understanding of book types	Showing understanding of book types; attempt to explain the author's book type	Showing deep understanding of book types; author's books well explained
Locate and provide personal details about the author.	Lacking evidence of research Not in own words	Well researched Information mostly in own words	Well researched information, written in own words Well written Detail provided
Provide other interesting information or illustrations.	One extra piece of information or an illustration	Two pieces of information with some explanation or an outstanding illustration	Two or more pieces of extra information, or illustrations with detailed explanations
2. Character study			
Complete a character web.	Selected adjectives Limited information in accounts to explain character	Well selected adjectives Accounts explain character well	Interesting adjectives Detailed, well written accounts to explain character

Name: ....

Activity	Low	Medium	High
3. Characters' emotions			
What emotions do the characters show?	Showing limited understanding of emotions	Small range of emotions selected	A range of emotions carefully selected
How does the author develop these emotions or feelings?	Limited knowledge of development of emotions; an attempt at an explanation	Beginning to identify the strategies used by the author to develop emotions; explained clearly	Author's strategies to develop character emotions identified and explained
Find a passage in which the author uses words skilfully to develop feelings.	Passage chosen	Appropriate passage that explains emotions chosen	Highly appropriate passage, detailing emotional development, chosen
4. Choice of descriptive passage			
Choose a book passage (half a page or more).	Small passage chosen	Descriptive passage chosen	Highly descriptive passage of sufficient length chosen
What strategies has the author used to make this description come alive for you?	Attempt to explain why this passage is appealing	Explanation of why the passage holds interest; attempt to explain the author's strategies	Interesting aspects of passage and author strategies clearly explained
5. What does the author do in the books that shows she/he is Australian?	Attempt at identifying what makes the writing Australian	Parts of the writing showing that the author is Australian identified, or absence of this evidence identified	Parts of the writing showing that the author is Australian identified and explained, or absence of this evidence identified and explained
6. Presentation			
Present your study in poster form, and in your reading book.	Presented in readable, usable fashion	Readable and usefully organised presentation	Presented in a highly readable, usable way, and illustrated

Explicit teaching

Writing a book review

Students are often asked to write a book review. Very often, this ends up as a recount of the story with a very basic opinion at the end, such as: "It was fun to read", and perhaps a score out of ten. Most often, there are no criteria upon which to base the opinion or score. I made the decision some time ago that this type of response was not achieving a great deal. All it did was assure the teacher that the student had read the book.

Once I had reached that decision, my next task was to find excellent reviews of children's books. This did not prove easy. As it happened, the best were to be found in places where children's literature was reviewed for teachers, so I used these, explaining to the students that teachers formed the intended audience.

Lesson 1

First, the teacher must explain that a book review is a particular genre that is not just a recount. Students then listen to several book reviews that demonstrate the best of this genre. I have provided a good example under — a review of Gary Crew's *Bright Star*, written by Meredith Costian for *Classroom* magazine.

Something different once again from the innovative Gary Crew, *Bright Star* is the story of Alicia, a farmer's daughter, who discovers that life is full of rich possibilities that, like space, have no limits.

Set in rural Australia in the late nineteenth century, the book provides an opportunity to examine how gender roles and expectations have changed over time; the boys Alicia knows are given the freedom of choice and encouraged to continue their schooling, while she is expected to fill her time with endless chores and needlework. She compares herself to a 'plodding cow' and the boys to 'swallows' free to come and go as they please. And then she meets the 'Star Man', an astronomer who comes to her school and introduces her to not only a world of comets and planets, but to the realisation that change is "a choice only you can make".

Although Alicia is a fictional character, the 'Star Man' is in fact an amateur astronomer from Windsor, New South Wales, who achieved astronomical fame by discovering The Great Comet of 1861. Anne Spudvilas' portrait-like illustrations and the elegant old-fashioned typeface help reinforce the book's historical basis.

Students are asked to identify the structure and techniques that give the required information while holding the reader's interest. The structure that was identified in my classroom in the year of writing was:

Paragraph 1

Author, title and main character are introduced in an attention-grabbing style. A small hint is given about the story.

Paragraph 2

The plot is investigated in a little more depth. The setting and perhaps the era are explained. Any issues that can be identified are discussed. The characters and their problems are briefly introduced.

Paragraph 3

Any interesting extras that are known about the author or characters can be added. Illustrations are explained/discussed.

Paragraph 4

Another paragraph of opinion or recommendation could be an optional extra.

The pattern is made into a 'features list' and is posted in the classroom.

The students return to the reviews to investigate tense and modality. Together, we identify that:

◆ the present tense of book reviews gives an immediacy that helps to capture the interest of the reader; it also suggests that the writer has a good knowledge of the book in review and has perhaps just finished reading it

◆ the modality of a review indicates the writer's view of the book; the higher the modality, the stronger the opinion and the recommendation. (Here we might consider the description of a book as a 'must read' — a high-modality expression that tells readers that the book will prove very enjoyable.)

Students then attempt to write an attention-grabbing introductory paragraph about the book that they have chosen to review. Once they are satisfied with their attempts, volunteers are called to share their writing. Comments or suggestions are called for, and further time is allowed for changes to be incorporated.

Lesson 2

Students are reminded about some of the decisions made in the previous lesson. The lesson is then devoted to writing the review. Throughout the lesson, time is called for sharing, with students asked to volunteer where they are up to at that moment, or to read out the best sentence they have written. As the lesson progresses, the students give and receive a variety of feedback, enabling them to build both their writing and reviewing skills. I also like to reinforce the idea that it is important to read over work as you go, and to make corrections in draft writing.

The students often need a homework session on top of these two lessons. Once finished, the review becomes part of each student's 'author study' poster.

Jodie's Journey by world-renowned, prize winning author Colin Thiele captures the lifestyle of living in the South Australian Hills, *bush fire country*, while telling the story of a courageous young girl, Jodie, whose love of her horse pulls her through a life of problems and tragedies not faced by most ordinary Australian children.

This is Colin Thiele's thirty eighth children's book. He was inspired by a young girl, Sharyn Stevens', letter written to him and telling him about the crippling disease they shared, and asking if he could write a book to tell others about it. This book is result of that letter. He also had help from another young sufferer, Charmain Hodge, while his daughter, Sandy, a horse lover and keen rider provided much of the information about horses and horse riding. It was then handed to Dr Stephen Milazzo, who checked the accurateness of it's medical content. It combines real life places and happenings, while the actual towns and characters are fictitious. this is done so superbly you will feel like you are there and will not want to put this book down!

This novel tells about the pain suffered not only by Jodie but also that suffered by her friends, family and even her foes. It also tells about the horrific Ash Wednesday fires and the destruction left when the fire was eventually put to rest.

This fantastic book shows that whatever problems you face there is always someone worse and with time, effort and determination any problems can be conquered. It is perfect for children of around ten to twelve years of age, although the concept and the gripping story line provide a compelling read and lesson for someone of any age group.

Read it and you will not be left feeling disappointed or uncontent.

Julia's review of Jodie's Journey *by Colin Thiele.*

Investigating characters' emotions

The emotions of characters are not always easy for students to identify, but this is a necessary skill if students are to write characters successfully themselves. Very often, an author builds a character throughout a book, developing the character's reactions to situations and to other characters and writing about the emotions experienced.

Some authors do this better (or with greater emphasis) than others. While some authors put more emphasis on plot, others develop their characters or describe settings expertly. One Australian author who always provides me with excellent modelling for development of characters' emotions is Colin Thiele.

The following is generally completed in one lesson.

The class jointly discusses what is meant by 'characters' emotions'. Students are prompted to offer words describing a range of emotions. These can be referred to subsequently as a vocabulary resource. The words are listed on large paper for posting in the classroom. Some examples are:

antagonistic	sad	frustrated	annoyed	overjoyed
depressed	miserable	unhappy	dejected	low-spirited
down	upset	disturbed	bothered	perturbed
discouraged	infuriated	exasperated	wound up	aggressive
hostile	gloomy	cheerless	distressed	disappointed
friendly	content	pleased	glad	joyful
happy	cheerful	blissful	high-spirited	delighted
ecstatic	jubilant	elated	triumphant	satisfied

Once these have been listed, the teacher reads out a selected passage that is displayed via an overhead transparency. (I often use the following passage from *Jodie's Journey* (Thiele, 1990), but there are many more; choose from the book you may be reading to your class, a book that one of your students is reading, or something that catches your students' interest. For further ideas, *Kids Best* (PETA, 2000) is recommended. In your reading, take care to bring the passage to life.)

The students jointly identify the words, phrases and sentences that provide clues to the characters' emotions. (I have underlined the phrases that, as a class, we identified.)

In the yard at recess time, as she and Tanya sat sharing an apple, dozens of their schoolmates came up to talk about <u>Jodie's win</u>. They did it in all kinds of ways.

"It was a <u>magic ride Jode</u> ..."

"Can I borrow your horse, Carpo?"

"What about a loan, money bags?"

<u>Jodie beamed</u>. Because she was so small — "like a dark haired little gypsy girl" old Bert Martin used to say — she had never stood out in sport or leadership at school. It was nice <u>to be top dog</u> for a change, <u>to be a winner</u>. She <u>basked in the glow</u> of it.

Only Amanda Ritchie and a few of her clique failed to congratulate her. "I don't know how she does it," Amanda said loudly, <u>talking with her head in the air</u>. There was a brief pause. Everyone was silent, wondering what she meant, which was exactly what Amanda wanted so that she could attract attention. "I reckon she puts glue on the rails to stop them falling."

Although Amanda was a big girl it seemed for a moment that <u>Jodie was going to fly at her</u>. <u>Her dark eyes shone angrily</u>. "Some riders are just plain clumsy," <u>she answered sarcastically</u>. It was a barbed reference to one of Amanda's recent rides when she had spreadeagled most of the jumps on the course.

<u>Amanda's lip curled</u>. "And like I said, some people are plain tinny."

<u>Tanya stood up</u> at that. She was tall and blonde, with blue eyes and fair skin, like a girl from Sweden or Norway. "Look Amanda," she said, "<u>why don't you just rack off. If you're jealous of Jodie then go and cry in a bucket.</u>" It was a comment that was too honest and too forthright for Amanda. She <u>huffed in disdain and walked away</u>.

For the rest of the week <u>Jodie was still on top of the world</u>. On Saturday she had a lovely party for her twelfth birthday. Tanya, Lynn Abbott and two or three other close friends stayed on and slept overnight, talking in bed until two o'clock in the morning and then sleeping in luxuriously. But the soreness in Jodie's hands and the pain in her knees and hips didn't improve. <u>She felt achy and out of sorts</u>.

Source: Thiele, C (1990), Jodie's Journey. *Reprinted with permission of Lothian Books.*

In this passage, the contrast between Jodie and Amanda is quite marked. Thiele uses this contrast to highlight Jodie's feelings, enabling the reader to develop a much greater feeling for her character. These types of contrasts are usually well observed by the students.

Using the chosen passage, the class starts to generate a list of emotions that the chosen character displays. The students support their suggestions with a specific phrase or a combination of phrases from the text. For example, Jodie feels:

- joy   (*Jodie was still on top of the world*)

- elation   (*She basked in the glow of it*)

- anger   (*Her dark eyes shone angrily*)

- uneasiness   (*She felt achy and out of sorts*).

Thiele portrays these feelings with the language he chooses to show the state of Jodie's mind, by contrasting Jodie with Amanda, and by describing the actions of the two girls. To be able to highlight these features and strategies in a small passage is a great enabler for students and their writing.

With the lesson complete, students are asked to complete the assignment activity about characters' emotions (see page 49).

Australian writing

If students are to develop a sense of what is 'Australian writing' — as opposed to writing that emerges from other contexts — they will need to clarify their understanding of what is Australian. Although many will have a firmly held opinion, most will not have been expected to articulate it.

This unit asks students to express their thoughts about 'What is Australian?' and to investigate whether stereotyping is always a negative practice, or if it might sometimes have merit. It is expected that students will come to these lessons with some understanding of stereotyping; if not, some discussion about this concept will be necessary.

Lesson 1

Individually, students are asked to respond to the question: 'What does the term "Australian" mean to you?' Students enter their response in their reading book for further reference. They do not show what they have written to anyone else, but may use the ideas in the following group discussion.

Collaborative groups then form. In my class, there are set groups for this type of activity that change each term. I select the groups, considering a mix of gender and personality type. Each time these groups are formed, students take a turn in a particular role — leader, recorder, reporter or timekeeper. We have developed a features list for these roles, which is posted in the classroom. I maintain the groups for a term so that students can learn to work together and understand each other in depth. At other times, however, students may choose their own groups.

In their collaborative groups, the students are asked to brainstorm the question: 'What attributes are Australian?'. A time is set, usually 10–15 minutes, for the class to reconvene.

With the whole class back together, the elected reporters present each group's response. From these reports, a class list of 'Australian attributes' is compiled. All students need to be satisfied with this list, which is then posted in the classroom.

A further question can now be posed to the class group: 'Which of these attributes are stereotypical?'. Before they respond, it is important that students understand that a stereotype:

◆ generalises attributes that have been identified in the past

◆ is built up over time

◆ can refer to people, places and situations

◆ often has positive or negative connotations.

Those attributes considered to be stereotypical are marked on the list. There are many different stereotypes for a single category. For example, the cork hat, the 'bushie', the 'bronzed Aussie surfie' and the 'wide brown land' may all be considered stereotypical. The stereotypes are marked on the list and discussed in comparison with those attributes that are not considered to be stereotypical.

Lesson 2

For this lesson, students are asked to come prepared, having selected a character they know well from a novel, and whom they are able to discuss.

At the beginning of the lesson, each student is asked to list the attributes of the chosen character. Students need to be clear and explicit in their listing, including physical as well as emotional attributes and interests.

In pairs, students then compare their character lists with the class-devised list from the previous lesson, in order to decide whether the characters they have chosen have 'Australian' character attributes. Partners decide this together, then combine with another pair to share their findings.

In the final part of this lesson, students return to their reading-book responses to the original question: 'What does the term "Australian" mean to you?'. They read these again, making any alterations or additions that they now feel would be appropriate.

To conclude the lesson, the class group discusses the question: 'What will you look for in a novel to identify whether it is written by an Australian author?'. This is a purely oral brainstorming session, used by the students to reflect on this section of their work. Individual reflections are then recorded using a right-angled graphic organiser (opposite), which students complete individually for inclusion in their portfolio.

What is Australian?

What will you look for?

....

....

....

....

Feelings

....

....

....

....

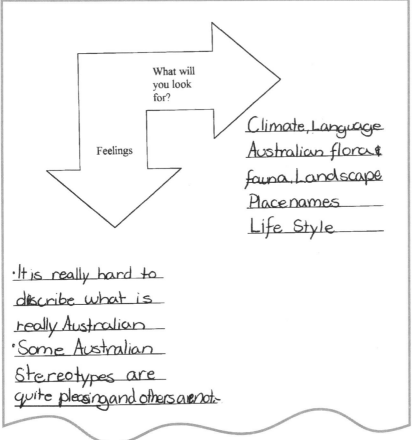

What will you look for?

Feelings

Climate, Language
Australian flora &
fauna, Landscape
Place names
Life Style

· It is really hard to
describe what is
really Australian
· Some Australian
Stereotypes are
quite pleasing and others are not.

Gaynor's reflection on the meaning of 'Australian', indicating the aspects she will consider in identifying whether a novelist's work is Australian.

Development of setting

The development of the setting of a novel is usually more easily understood than characterisation. However, it is still not an easy task for student writers. For this reason, it is important to provide good models. Colin Thiele has a fine touch, as does Patricia Wrightson. In the following passages, words are used skilfully to develop vivid mental images of the places described. By way of contrast, I have selected scenes in very different environments — seaside, outback, city.

In this one-lesson session, students receive a print-out of the passages, then follow each one as I read it aloud. They are asked to picture the scenes in their minds.

Storm Boy lived between the Coorong and the sea. His home was the long, long snout of sandhill and scrub that curves away south-eastwards from the Murray Mouth. A wild strip it is, windswept and tussocky, with the flat shallow water of the South Australian Coorong on one side and the endless slam of the Southern Ocean on the other. They call it the Ninety Mile Beach. From thousands of miles round the cold, wet underbelly of the world the waves come sweeping in towards the shore and pitch down in a terrible ruin of white water and spray. All day and all night they tumble and thunder, and when the wind rises it whips the sand up the beach and the white spray darts and writhes in the air like snakes of salt.

Source: Thiele, C (1976) Storm Boy. *Rigby, Adelaide. Reprinted with kind permission of New Holland Publishers.*

The opal fields lay six hundred miles north-west of Adelaide, midway between Port Augusta and Alice Springs. A flat, bare landscape it was for the most part, with undulations here and there and flat-topped hills and break-aways and wind-swept plains. An old old land, eroded and wrinkled, worn down over endless ages, peneplain on peneplain, until even the hills were remnants of ancient plains. And in the sides of the slopes, cut into every knoll and knob, were doorways and entrances and burrows as if the whole place was inhabited by five-foot-high rabbits walking about on their hind legs.

These were the dugouts — cheap, convenient homes that were warm in the winter and cool in summer and never needed painting. Every room was hacked out of the natural sandstone, the walls and roof often beautifully marked and stippled in natural colour — cream and ochre and red-brown — as if interior decorators had been called in to deck the place out in mottled patterns.

Source: Thiele, C (1981) The Fire in the Stone. *Reprinted with permission of Penguin Books Australia.*

Andy Hoddel stood on the pavement in Blunt Street and watched his friends taking turns on a skate-board. The street went plunging downhill into a deep hollow and rose steeply again beyond it. On this side of the street, the pavement ran down under high blank walls; on the opposite side, a row of quaint old cottages tipped downhill with the street. The cottages were clumsy and ugly, squashed together in terraces, and each with a tiny square of front garden. To make up for their sameness and their squat, narrow ugliness they were all painted different colours: sooty blue, grimy green, pink fading to yellow, white turning grey. They all wore television antennae like crazy parasols on their roofs.

Source: Wrightson, P (1971) I Own the Racecourse! *Puffin, Melbourne. Permission granted by the copyright owner c/- Curtis Brown (Aust.) P/L.*

Once the passages have been read and any of the more difficult words discussed (*peneplain*, for example), the students are asked to picture the scenes in their minds. A discussion follows, prompted by focus questions such as:

- If you were standing in the scene, what would you be seeing?

- How would you be feeling?

- What would you be experiencing?

- What sort of area is this?

- What sort of people would be living here?

- Is this a rich or poor area?

- How far could you see?

- What words allow you to answer these questions so accurately?

A further set of questions can focus discussion of the mental pictures that these passages evoke:

- What colours do you see?

- Are there roads? What do they look like?

- What other things impress you about the scene you are able to picture?

Every class group responds differently to such questions, but all students see and feel something when presented with evocative passages such as these.

After the class discussion, students divide into groups to write their own passage about a familiar scene. I find that it is usually productive to provide a small list of scenes from which students may choose; it is important that they are not held back if they can't decide on a setting. Some suggestions might be: your own bedroom; the street where you live; the school yard.

This session not only supports the students in selecting descriptive writing from the novels they read, it also pays dividends in their own writing.

Types of books

Books can be categorised in many ways. The broad categories of fiction and non-fiction do not meet the needs of this assignment, and more refined classification is needed. Ideas that enable this refinement can be generated in the following activity, which takes only one lesson to complete.

In preparing for this lesson, I ask students to come with the novel — and any other books — that they are reading at the time. I bring a selection of books by Australian authors. This provides a wide variety of books to identify.

Using the books that I have sourced, we start a list identifying types of books. Some recommended books are:

◆ the *Tomorrow* series by John Marsden — war fiction

◆ *Raw* by Scott Monk — social comment

◆ *Blue Fin* by Colin Thiele — adventure/family relationships/sea

◆ *Came Back to Show You I Could Fly* by Robin Klein — social comment/ drugs

◆ *Looking for Alibrandi* by Melina Marchetta — social comment/family

◆ *Plastic City* by Margaret Clark — environmental comment

◆ *Playing Beatie Bow* by Ruth Park — time travel/Australian history

◆ *The River Kings* by Max Fatchen — historical fiction

◆ *Boss of the Pool* by Robin Klein — disability

◆ *Space Demons* by Gillian Rubinstein — science fiction

◆ *Don't Pat the Wombat* by Elizabeth Honey — school story

◆ *Seven Little Australians* by Ethel Turner — historical/classic.

There is a multitude of books from which to choose, and many excellent Australian authors. It is important to choose a variety of different types and styles.

In a class discussion, we look at each book and decide what type of book each one could be called. Students who have read these books are a good source of information, and my input is necessary. This process has two very important outcomes: the category list is compiled; and new books are introduced, from which students may choose as part of their assignment.

(You may note that the book 'types' listed above are not of a kind; 'science fiction', for example, is a genre classification, whereas 'disability' is thematic. However, the purpose of this activity is to open up the diverse approaches that writers take.)

Students then form groups of four or five. Together, they work out the types of books that they have brought to the lesson.

The class then reconvenes, and groups add any different book types to the list, which is charted and posted in the classroom.

At this point, the students are able to continue the assignment with an expanded list of book types. They have also had the opportunity to talk about books that have been recommended by both the teacher and their peers.

A good start for a list of book types is:

Fiction	Non-fiction
Fantasy: science fiction, time travel, fairy tales, animal fiction	Picture book
	Story
Tradition: community stories, Dreaming stories	Encyclopedia
	Humour
Mystery: detective, adventure	Comic format
Family: relationships, grandparents, brothers and sisters	Newspaper format
	Biography
History: war, holocaust, historical romance	Sport
Friendship: teenage	Report/Review
Humour	Statistics
Adventure	
Romance	
Social comment	

Assessment

Assessment for this assignment is done once the whole assignment is completed near the end of the term. One copy of the rubric is printed for each student and I use this to make my assessment. Looking at the rubric and reading the work, I match the outcomes and put a highlighter line through the level of achievement I believe the student has attained. My students often ask for a mark or grade because they are insistent that their parents ask for this. In this case I allocate scores to each level of the continuum and add these at the end. While I do not always advocate scoring and grading, giving a numerical value to negotiated outcomes seems to have more merit than the assessor allocating a score or grade on his/her own criteria.

Assessment reflection

This term's program supports all students in both reading and writing.

The rubric offers one of the major means of support, providing both a target to work towards and a clear outline of assessment criteria. Students feel an ownership of these criteria, having negotiated them with their teacher. Because the rubric is negotiated in the early part of the unit, it is very streamlined when marking time arrives, enabling each student's work to be marked thoroughly in a minimum of time.

Preparation for term 3

So that they are prepared for term 3's assignment, I ask the students to select a novel that they would like to study in depth. This book must have a strong story line, identifiable issues and suitable length — I use the words "a depth of story" and "meatiness" to get my message across.

These books will need to be chosen and discussed about three weeks before the end of this term to allow sufficient time for each student to complete her/his reading before term 3 commences. This is important, because term 3's assignment work needs to begin in the first week of that term.

References

Costian, M (1996) Review in *Classroom* magazine, Scholastic Australia, Sydney.

Crew, G (1996) *Bright Star.* Lothian Books, Melbourne.

Fatchen, M (1980) *The River Kings.* Methuen Children's Books, London.

Clark, M (1992) *Plastic City.* Random House, Sydney.

Honey, E (1996) *Don't Pat the Wombat.* Allen & Unwin, Sydney.

Kids Best: Australian Books for Children and Young Adults 1996–2000. Primary English Teaching Association, Sydney, 2000.

Klein, R (1986) *Boss of the Pool.* Omnibus Books, Adelaide.

Klein, R (1992) *Came Back to Show You I Could Fly.* Narkaling Productions, Perth.

Marchetta, M (1993) *Looking for Alibrandi.* Penguin, Melbourne.

Marsden, J (1993) *Tomorrow, When the War Began.* Pan Macmillan, Sydney.

Monk, S (1988) *Raw.* Random House Australia, Sydney.

Park, R (1987) *Playing Beatie Bow.* Angus & Robertson, Sydney.

Rubinstein, G (1986) *Space Demons.* Omnibus Books, Adelaide.

Thiele, C (1978) *Blue Fin.* Rigby, Adelaide.

Thiele, C (1990) *Jodie's Journey.* Walter McVitty Books, Sydney.

Thiele, C (1976) *Storm Boy.* Rigby, Adelaide.

Thiele, C (1981) *The Fire in the Stone.* Puffin, Harmondsworth, UK.

Turner, E (1912) *Seven Little Australians.* (1991) Angus & Robertson, Sydney.

Wrightson, P (1971) *I Own the Racecourse!* Puffin, Melbourne.

term three

1
2
3
4

Chapter 5: A closer look at a book

Planning

With two terms of assignment work behind them, students have developed a deeper understanding of:

◆ issues in texts

◆ authors' styles

◆ elements of good writing.

In term 3, students are required to study a book of their choice, in depth. This is a term's assignment, the details of which are determined by each individual, building on the skills developed during the previous terms. Again, time management is an issue that needs support and reminders; however, because the assignment tasks are self-determined, each student is highly aware of the time constraints and is motivated to take greater control.

The explicit teaching in this term is about asking questions — opening up a book to find issues that might otherwise pass unnoticed. Because the students do take control of their own learning, they demonstrate great effort and pride in what they present. This assignment is often a high point in their year.

Targeted outcomes

The specific outcomes targeted in this term differ from those of the previous terms. Students:

◆ investigate one book in depth, looking at various issues and using the book as a starting point to further develop their own thinking, creating and evaluating

◆ develop a set of questions with varying levels of complexity for a reading assignment

◆ develop higher-order thinking skills

◆ present findings in an oral presentation which demonstrates learning, organisation and creativity.

While these outcomes are firmly rooted in band B of the national English statement and profile, this style of assignment often motivates students to achieve at a higher level than assignments generated by the teacher. Therefore, students are often seen to be moving well into band C with their outcomes.

To achieve these outcomes, I teach the following areas explicitly:

◆ Using a question matrix

◆ Setting tasks using Bloom's taxonomy of questioning

◆ Oral presentation.

This assignment is structured differently from the previous two, with explicit teaching occurring at the beginning, rather than throughout the term.

Introducing the assignment

At the end of the previous term, I asked the students to choose a book for study in this term. I made this request about three weeks before the term's end, so that all students had sufficient time to read the book by the beginning of term 3.

I provided the students with clear criteria for their selection — that is, that their selected book must be:

◆ a novel that they have not previously read

◆ appropriate to their reading ability

◆ of sufficient depth or 'meatiness' to support a term-long study

◆ interesting to the student

◆ one that contains issues about which the student will be able to speak to the gathered class group in an oral presentation

◆ approved by the teacher or librarian by the end of term 2.

Students rise to this request; choosing the novel becomes a task that is undertaken with interest, enjoyment and skill. At this age, students often find that they are developing an interest in teenage fiction, and I encourage this.

It is often wise to discuss a book's back-cover 'blurb' with the student. When issues of love, sex and/or death are contained in the chosen story, the student must be aware of the fact that they may need to address these sensitive topics in the oral presentation.

I record a list of the books chosen by the students. Further negotiation is needed to change this. This record gives the students a feeling of formality and underlines the importance of having the book read in time for the assignment.

Together, the class views and considers the elements of the 'Term 3 reading assignment' (see following).

Term 3 reading assignment

Task

Complete an in-depth book study to be presented to the class.

Make sure that you have read the book that you selected and recorded last term.

1. With your teacher, fill out the focusing matrix sheet to ensure that you have thought deeply and clearly about the book.

2. Using the matrix and the 'Book study' sheet, set the tasks for your own assignment, taking into account your interests and the issues in the book you have read.

3. Complete the tasks you have set for yourself; be aware of the presentation you choose, as you will need to show the audience what you have done and explain all your work.

4. Invite a significant adult to attend when you present your work to the class. This person may be a parent or grandparent, family friend or another teacher, eg librarian, principal or deputy principal.

5. Present your work to the class in an oral presentation, then give all the materials to your teacher for completion of assessment.

Presentation

- Inform your audience about the book that you studied, explaining why you chose it and why it was a good choice or not.

- Read an extract from the book. This must be long enough for the audience to understand the passage you have selected. A minimum of two pages is suggested. You will be assessed on your oral reading.

- Present the findings of your study.

- Show all your work to the class, including the matrix and the 'Book study' sheet.

- Present all illustrations and models.

- If you have prepared any performances, make sure that these are performed in some way.

- Read the most interesting piece of writing you have produced for this assignment.

- Summarise how you went about your work and in what ways you extended your knowledge and abilities.

- Report on your time management.

- State the number of points you scored for the tasks you set.

An Explicit Reading Program

Communicating with parents

 Once again, I keep parents informed about the reading happenings in the classroom, alerting them to what they might expect from their children. It is also important to ensure that parents are regularly invited into the classroom so that they really feel that they are part of the partnership of their children's learning.

Dear Parent,

I hope you have been as impressed with your child's reading assignment as I have been with the effort and accomplishments achieved by the class as a whole. The book reviews have been particularly outstanding. All the assignments are displayed in the classroom; if you have some time, drop in and look at them — and be impressed!

Last term, I asked the students to read a specially chosen book before they returned to school this term. During this week we will complete a question matrix that will help to focus students' thoughts about the book and require them to think about it deeply. They will bring this home to you later in the week; some may need to put some finishing touches to it for homework.

The next stage of the assignment will require students to construct their own questions about the book. There is an ideas sheet to help them develop these questions; you will be able to see these completed by week 2. Students will then work to answer the questions they have set. To complete their assignment, they will present their findings to the class in the final weeks of the term. They will invite an adult to be part of their audience.

Once again, your child will need support with time management, although I can see that all students are making great progress in this area and will have a better idea of what is required. We will use the diary to set weekly and nightly goals; you can expect to find information there that will keep you updated.

Thank you for your continued support.

Regards

Kerry Gehling

Presentation requirements

The students may choose their own methods of presenting their work. The only stipulation is that it must be able to be displayed during their oral presentation. Many choose to key in their writing and present print-outs in a display book. Others continue to use their reading (exercise) books; a few use overhead projector transparencies or PowerPoint presentations. This choice depends on the skills of the individual. On occasion, small plays have been presented and scripts have been taped and played back to the class.

When I introduce the assignment outline as above (p 71), the question of presentation is always a topic for discussion. It is important for students to be able to present in an attractive way, but they need to be careful not to let the presentation become so complicated that it detracts from the work they have done. Closer to the end of term, I provide explicit teaching about presentation skills. This results in a wall-displayed features list for students to refer to.

Explicit teaching

Using a question matrix

Early in week 1 of this term, students are reminded that their book reading must be completed. In the middle of the week, they are presented with a question matrix, developed after the work of Wiederhold (1995) (see p 18). This matrix is designed to focus the students on aspects of the book that they may not have considered at any depth. Hereon, we refer to this as the 'focusing matrix' in the classroom.

Students are not required to answer the questions on the matrix; however, they may choose to use ideas generated by the focusing questions. The matrix is explained carefully, showing the two elements that must be taken into account when posing a question for any one box. To become familiar with the process that the students will go through, I advise teachers to first use the matrix to devise their own set of questions for a book that they know.

A Year in Texts

Name:

Date:

Develop questions that will support you to consider, in depth, the book that you have read.

Jot down ideas that will help you construct your own assignment.

	Event	Situation	Choice	Person	Reason	Means
Present	What is?	Where/When is?	Which is?	Who is?	Why is?	How is?
Past	What did?	Where/When did?	Which did?	Who did?	Why did?	How did?
Possibility	What can?	Where/When can?	Which can?	Who can?	Why can?	How can?
Probability	What would?	Where/When would?	Which would?	Who would?	Why would?	How would?
Prediction	What will?	Where/When will?	Which will?	Who will?	Why will?	How will?
Imagination	What might?	Where/When might?	Which might?	Who might?	Why might?	How might?

The question or focusing matrix that my students use to generate questions that will assist them to interrogate a chosen text.

I explain that the vertical elements — present, past, possibility, probability, prediction and imagination — lead the question setter from simple thought about the book to more complex thought that should take them beyond the book, requiring imagination and creativity:

◆ Present: What is happening in the book?

◆ Past: What led up to the happenings in the book, or what happened to make the characters act as they did?

◆ Possibility: Considering what you now know about the book, what things *might* happen to the characters, plot and issues in the book?

◆ Probability: Considering what you now know about the book, what things are *likely* to happen?

◆ Prediction: What do you think the longer-term future holds for the book's characters, events or issues? This must be built on what you have found out from the book.

◆ Imagination: Take your thoughts further, and imagine what else you might uncover if you think deeply about the book's characters, events and issues. This might involve the past, present or future.

We then look at the horizontal elements of the matrix — events, situations, choices, people, reasons and means. These organisers help to focus students' thoughts on the aspects and issues that may be developed in the story. They are quite easy for students to understand, and link well with the vertical elements.

Once the elements are explained, I lead the class through each question box, giving an example for each. The students write a question on their own copy of the matrix. As the boxes are completed, I walk around the classroom to check and to select questions that provide good examples to read out. I have collected examples from previous years and I also use these to provide a wide variety of good examples.

Often, part way through the lesson — even though I have explained its purpose — students ask: "If this isn't the assignment, why are we doing it?". My answer is always: "Are you having to think really hard about your book?". The answers always come back as vigorous nods.

This is a focusing exercise which ensures that all students have thought about plot, characterisation and setting in their chosen book. Although all students fill in the same box at the same time, not one of them develops the same question as another.

When the students have filled in their matrices, I check them carefully to ensure that each box has a question, and that each question shows the student has understood both the task and the question type.

An Explicit Reading Program

Who is? — Who is Rowan going to be friends with after the quest?

Why is? — Why is it important for Rowan to join the party?

Who did? — Who did dislike Rowan ... during the quest?

Why did? — Why did Rowan join the party?

Who can? — Who can go on to finish the quest?

Why can? — Why can the party see people in their minds?

Who would? — Who would believe in Rowan from now on?

Why would? — Why would the party go on the quest?

Who will? — Who will be able to kill the dragon if trouble strikes again?

Why will? — Why will Rowan believe in himself more?

Who might? — Who might be the bravest people in the work?

Why might? — Why might people who help bravely feel that they have not REALLY been brave?

Person   Reason

Where/When is? — Where is the mountain situated in relation to Rin?

Which is? — Which is more important, your life or an animal?

Where/When did? — When did the climbing party start trusting and liking Rowan?

Which did? — Which choice did Rowan take. To go on or to turn back?

Where/When can? — Where can Rowan hide from the dragon if necessary?

Which can? — Which decision can Strong John take after the tunnel?

Where/When would? — Where would the bukshah be able to go to if Rowan failed?

Which would? — Which decision would the party have made if Rowan wasn't there?

Where/When will? — When will Rowan need to go on another?

Which will? — Which people will like or dislike Rowan after the quest?

Where/When might? — When might have the party started to give up without Rowan?

Which might? — Which might be more scary, going on the quest or fighting the dragon?

Situation   Choice

A sample from Charlotte's completed question matrix.

Setting tasks

Once the question matrix has been completed, students are presented with the 'Book study' pro forma (opposite) that will form the basis for developing their assignment questions and tasks. This grid is based on Bloom's taxonomy of questioning. I explain to the students that the taxonomy is a hierarchy of thinking skills that builds from simple factual knowledge to more complex thinking and creating.

The development of thinking from lower to higher levels is an important aspect of this model. This is reflected in the scoring system. When students set themselves a task from the knowledge and comprehension sections, they score one point for a lower level of thinking; by setting tasks from the application or analysis sections, they score two points; and by setting tasks from the synthesis or evaluation sections, they score four points. Students must score at least 30 points, with a minimum from each section. This is briefly outlined on the pro forma, but acts only as a reminder and needs to be fully explained to the students in an introduction.

Book study

Name: ....

Date: ....

An Explicit Reading Program

continued....

Assignment points

Minimum required   30 points

See the point explanation for guidelines.

Point explanation

Assignment must include:
4 tasks from K & C
3 tasks from A & A
2 tasks from S & E.

This gives you 18 points. Make this up to 30 from any section.

	Useful verbs	Activities	Task stems	Assignment tasks
Knowledge 1 point	Tell List Describe Relate Locate Write Find State Name	List all the main events. Make a timeline. Make a fact chart. List all the characters. Chart some information. Write a poem.	What happened after ...? How many ...? Who was it that ...? Describe what happened ... Explain why ...	• • • • •
Comprehension 1 point	Explain Interpret Outline Discuss Distinguish Describe Predict Translate Compare	Illustrate an event. Illustrate the main idea. Draw a comic strip. Retell the story in your own words. Write a summary of one event. Present a flow chart. Make a colouring book.	Write in your own words ... Write a brief outline ... Who was the key character ...? What differences exist between ...? Provide a definition for ... What was the main idea ...?	• • • • •
Application 2 points	Solve Show Use Illustrate Calculate Construct Compute Classify Examine	Construct a model or diorama. Compile a scrap book. Collect pictures to demonstrate a point. Make a puzzle game. Dress a doll as a character. Paint a picture or mural.	Develop a set of instructions ... What questions would you ask of ...? Identify the issues raised ... What is the turning point ...? How do the characters relate to ...? What settings are used ...?	• • • • •

	Useful verbs	Activities	Task stems	Assignment tasks
Analysis 2 points	Analyse Distinguish Examine Compare Contrast Investigate Explain Separate Advertise Categorise	Write a commercial. Make a jigsaw puzzle. Make a family tree. Prepare an author study. Write a biography of a character.	If ____, what might have happened? Which events could not have really happened? Why did changes occur? What other endings might have been possible? What was the turning point in the story?	• • • • • • •
Synthesis 4 points	Create Invent Compose Predict Plan Construct Design Imagine Improve Propose	Invent a machine. Design a CD or video cover. Sell an idea. Design a building. Devise a way to …	Design a ____ which can … Compose a song about … What possible solution can you see to …? Devise a way to … What would happen if …? Create new uses for … Develop a menu for …	• • • • • • •
Evaluation 4 points	Judge Select Choose Decide Justify Argue Verify Discuss Recommend	Prepare a list of criteria. Present both sides of an argument. Prepare a set of rules and justify them. Write a letter.	Develop a better solution for … How would you feel if …? Defend your position about … Prepare notes for … Write a letter … What is your belief about …?	• • • • •

When introducing the 'Book study' pro forma, I read through each section as students jot down their first thoughts for assignment tasks. I recommend pencil be used in preference to pen, as tasks will often be changed before they are finally settled.

It is important to explain that the useful verbs, activity types and task stems on the pro forma need to be put together to determine the task that will eventually be set. It is also important to emphasise that this assignment is being set by the students themselves and that they should write questions that will increase their knowledge, challenge them and, importantly, interest them.

I have found it useful to explain the idea of rigour. For example, one popular task is to 'List the characters in the story'. I always suggest that an extra part be added to that task, so that it becomes: 'List characters in the story, and describe one characteristic of each'.

The setting of tasks needs to be discussed in detail. I provide some guidelines to consider:

◆ Set open-ended tasks; try to avoid tasks that answer questions beginning with 'Can/Does/Is'.

◆ Set tasks that are interesting for you to do.

◆ Make sure that the tasks are sufficiently rigorous.

◆ Make sure that you have scored sufficiently, as this will ensure that you have a spread of task types.

As I lead students through the pro forma, I find it useful to provide some sample tasks for ideas (see over). Posting these examples around the classroom has proved to be a great support for students as they work to set their own tasks.

Task-setting usually takes one lesson. Most students like to take the pro forma home to consider their tasks and to put the finishing touches to their work. It is useful to emphasise that this will be their whole term's work, so they need to be satisfied with what they have set.

Once the students are satisfied with their tasks, I proofread their work and suggest improvements in wording or in establishing rigour. Proposed changes must be explained and negotiated. All negotiations are finalised before the end of the second week so that there is sufficient time for the students to answer their questions, complete their tasks, and prepare and deliver their oral presentations.

Sample tasks

Knowledge/Comprehension

Develop a timeline of the major events in the story.

Describe the physical features of the main characters.

Draw an object that has a part to play in this story.

Write a phone conversation that may have occurred between two major characters.

Compare the attitudes of different characters to something that has happened in the story.

Make a colouring book showing the reactions and feelings of one character in each chapter of the book.

Application/Analysis

Identify one issue in the book, then find out how this is being dealt with in a real-world situation.

Create a diorama to illustrate one setting in the book you have chosen.

Design and make a poster to illustrate your support for an issue that arises in the book you have read.

Design and make a jigsaw puzzle that illustrates the turning point in the story.

Construct a 'family tree'-style web to show how the characters in the story relate to one another.

Describe other possible outcomes for this story.

Synthesis/Evaluation

Invent a machine that will help one of the characters do a specific task from the book.

Name five tracks of music that would be enjoyed by the main character in the story. Explain why you have chosen this music.

Design a video cover for use when this book is made into a film.

Write a letter to the editor putting forward your point of view about an issue named in this book.

Prepare notes that give both sides of an argument about one of the issues raised in the book.

How would you feel if you were the main character in the book: Would you react in the same way to the situations in the story? How would your reactions differ?

	#Describe the reactions of the people of Rin #when Rowan showed them the map. # #List the characters and describe their #feelings about the quest. # #Tell why Sheba chose Rowan to be part of #the quest. #
	#Write a brief outline of the main event #that appealed to you most. #Provide a definition for "bukshah" #Make a colouring book showing the reactions #and feelings of each character in different #parts of the story # #
)	#What questions would you ask of Sheba if #you were Rowan and if you were Strong John? # #Construct a boardgame showing the quest that #the party took. # # #
happened? happened'? n possible? ory?	#If Rowan hadn't joined the party,what might #have happened in the ending? # #Make a jigsaw puzzle showing Rowans reactions #towards the map # #Explain why Strong John does not want to take #Rowan when they go on the quest.
___ to …?	#Design a machine/aid that would have helped the #party climb the cliffs. # #Name the music that would be suitable if this #book was made into a movie. # #Use this music and design a C-D cover for it, #if it became a sound track. #
	#Explain why you think that Rowan going on the #quest was a good thing or a bad thing. Take #into account Rowan's life and how he feels, the #bukshah and the people of R # How

A sample from Charlotte's completed 'Book study' pro forma.

An Explicit Reading Program

Working support

Time is set aside each week for the students to work on their book study. At least three lessons and two homework periods are allocated each week, with more time made available near the end of term.

While they are working on their assignment, the students need support in the form of encouragement, proofreading, and presentation and time-management advice.

◆ Students need encouragement to ensure that they are confident in what they are writing, making and presenting.

◆ Proofreading supports and models the process of refinement, guiding students to produce work that is as good as it can be, and of which they can be proud. I often read out pieces that are of a high standard to give support and examples for other class members.

◆ Presentation needs to be monitored; I remind students of the fact that their work will need to be shown to their audience. I have found that students give each other support and ideas in this area.

◆ Time management becomes less of an issue in this term because of the previous terms' experiences, but because all students are doing different questions, it is not as easy to provide explicit teaching support. A priority pro forma (see below) is often a useful aid, especially for students who find prioritising difficult, and who become anxious when they are unable to break their work down into its smaller components.

Time management
List the outcomes you want to achieve this week, in priority order.

1	
2	
3	
4	
5	
6	
7	
8	
9	
10	

The most important support that the teacher can provide is to be available for conferencing whenever requests emerge, and to speak with each student about their assignment at least once a week. I keep a weekly class checklist on which I record the students who approach me, so that I can follow up those I haven't seen.

Oral presentation

As the due date for the assignment approaches, students need some explicit teaching about the structure of successful oral presentation. I devote one lesson to supporting this aspect.

The significant adult selected by each student needs to be invited, and allocated a time that is mutually convenient. Students negotiate a time that suits the class, then write an invitation specifying the time, place and expected duration of the presentation. Invitations are devised by each student, but must be shown to the teacher before they are sent.

In groups of three or four, students share ideas on structuring their presentations, given the requirements listed on the 'Term 3 reading assignment' sheet (p 71). These groups spend 15–20 minutes developing and recording their decisions. One person from each group is then asked to report back to the class. Suggestions are recorded on a large piece of paper.

Once all groups have reported, a class discussion identifies the most appropriate suggestions. Inappropriate suggestions are deleted. A list of presentation components is then compiled. An example follows.

Presentation

- Remember to welcome and seat your significant adult on arrival.

- Introduce yourself and welcome your audience.

- Show the focusing matrix and assignment questions.

- Show the book and explain your choice.

- Read a passage from the book, give a brief explanation of its plot, and say how you developed the issues suggested by the author.

- Read out the tasks you set yourself, and show the work that goes with each task.

- Read out a piece of your writing that you choose to share with the class, and explain why you chose that piece.

- Show and demonstrate any models you have devised.

- Present any performances that you have devised.

---

continued

- Explain how you organised yourself so that you could have everything completed and well presented on time.

- State the number of points you achieved when you set your tasks, so that the audience understands the levels of thinking you have applied.

- Thank your significant adult for coming, and ask for any questions and feedback.

- Show your significant adult out of the classroom, and say a personal thankyou to her/him for coming.

Once the presentation organisation is agreed, students brainstorm the requirements for an oral presenation. For my class, this is usually a revision, as several oral presentation tasks will typically have been completed and assessed before this point. The brainstorm identifies such requirements as:

- clarity

- fluency

- emphasis

- eye contact

- body language

- opening statement

- organisation of ideas

- conclusion.

These requirements are clarified and listed on the assessment sheet (see the 'Oral presentation' section, p 88). This ensures that all students are aware of the criteria to be applied when their presentation is assessed.

I post a booking sheet in the classroom so that students are able to check on their allocated time. This will often need to be changed as students negotiate with their significant adult to find a time suitable to both.

Fifteen minutes is allocated for each presentation, which allows time to seat the visitor, explain the procedure, listen to the presentation, receive feedback and see the visitor out before the next visitor arrives. Each student is given the 'Book study assessment' (see pp 87–89), which is used to check that all assessment aspects and criteria have been addressed.

Oral presentation: On the day

This checklist helps to organise a smoothly run presentation session.

◆ In the morning, write the names of presenters and their time slots on the board.

◆ Ensure that presenters have organised their significant adult to come at the correct time.

◆ At the beginning of the session, make sure all presenters have their materials on their desk in readiness. They should also provide you with their named 'Book study assessment' sheets.

◆ Check that the first student is ready to greet their invited adult, introduce that person to you and show them where to sit.

◆ Prime the subsequent presenters to watch for their significant adult and to slip out quietly and wait with the adult until the previous presenter has finished.

◆ Once the first student has presented, comment briefly, then ask for feedback and comments from the class and the significant adult.

◆ Thank the adult for coming, ensuring that the presenter sees this person out and makes his or her own thankyous.

◆ Receive the presenter's work and give her/him a 'Peer comments' sheet (see p 91), which lists the names of all class members. The student is responsible for checking off who heard the presentation and obtaining a comment from each listener. Initially, the sheet is passed around the class. Any gaps will need to be followed up by the student. Once all listeners have commented, this sheet is included, along with the 'Book study assessment' sheets, in the student's portfolio.

Assessment

This assignment is assessed in several parts, but is driven by the oral presentation. The 'Book study assessment' consists of three pages (see pp 87–89):

◆ The first page provides spaces for teacher comments about illustrations, three-dimensional models and writing, as well as notes on question-setting, time management, choice of book and extension of knowledge. These require small comments; I complete them during and after the presentation.

- Teacher scaling of the presentation itself and related comments go on page two:
  - Oral reading is scaled according to volume, expression, clarity, fluency and variation. Reading out loud is not always an easy task for students but I find that, if given the chance to choose and prepare their reading, all students are able to reach an acceptable standard. The choice of passage is also scaled to enable comment on this task, since it requires a great amount of thought.
  - Oral presentation itself is scaled according to voice, confidence, structure and overall impression.
- The third page provides space for student, teacher, significant adult and parent reflection.

A further page provides space for peer comment, as discussed above. Because of the time and effort expended on this assignment, and because of the ownership developed when students set their own assignments, the comments are usually very supportive. It is important that these supportive comments and constructive criticisms be recorded.

Poem Of Nudas Feelings

Revenge, revenge, revenge,
These words ran through my mind,
Anger, anger, anger,
Was all I felt inside.
Those posters plastered everywhere,
Have deeply hurt my pride,
The power he has over me,
Seems never to sub side.
He has ruined my reputation,
In a way that's so unjust,
What can I do to change my world,
If I don't I will be crushed.

Emma's poem, produced as part of her book study of Touch Me, *along with her later self-assessment.*

assessment

I enjoyed doing this work and spent lots of time working on it. I think my best bit of work is probably the poem I did on to what I would feel like in Nudas position

Book study assessment

Name: ....

Name of book studied: ....

Book read before the beginning of term?　　　　Yes [ ]　　No [ ]

Question matrix ....

....

Assignment tasks ....

....

Did you find your choice of book appropriate?　　Yes [ ]　　No [ ]

Why? ....

....

Illustrations

- Used to decorate and enhance presentation ....
- Added to information and understanding of writing ....
- An integral part of study ....
- Of a high standard ....
- Comment ....

Three-dimensional models

- Well constructed ....
- Show planning and thoughtful presentation ....
- Add to information about the book ....
- Demonstrate understanding of the plot ....
- Of a high standard ....
- Comment ....

Writing

- Uses well constructed sentences ....
- Develops ideas well ....
- Shows thoughtful planning...
- Writes in detail and at sufficient length ....
- Presents own point of view articulately ....
- Comment ....

Extension of knowledge ....

....

Time management...

Task-setting points scored ....

Oral reading and presentation

Name: ....

Oral reading

	Poor	Satisfactory	Excellent
Volume			
Expression			
Clarity			
Fluency			
Variation			

Choice of passage

Interesting			
Descriptive words			
Able to stand alone			
Thought-provoking			
Entertaining			

Teacher comment:

Oral presentation

Voice

	Poor	Satisfactory	Excellent
Clarity, ability to be heard			
Fluency			
Emphasis			

Confidence

Eye contact			
Stance			
Body language			
Coping with mistakes			

Structure

Opening			
Logic of progression			
Conclusion			

Overall

Preparation and planning			
Use of notes			
Appropriateness of language			
Knowledge of book			
Audience response			

Name: ....

Student self-assessment:

Teacher's descriptive comment:

Comment from significant adult:

Parent signature and comment:

BOOK STUDY ASSESSMENT

Name of book studied <u>My Father is Not a Comedian!</u>

Book read before the beginning of term   yes [✓]   no [ ]

Question matrix <u>Excellent - you have reached into the issues as well.</u>

Assignment questions <u>Excellent tasks which have kept you enjoying your work.</u>

Did you find your choice of book appropriate?   yes [✓]   no [ ]
Explain why <u>because I could think of lots of questions and I really enjoyed doing them.</u>

Teacher comment

Speaking a little louder would have helped, but the people at the back heard clearly and that was the aim, so well done.

Comment from Significant Adult

I WAS VERY IMPRESSED WITH REBECCA'S WHOLE PRESENTATION. IT SHOWED SHE HAD WORKED VERY HARD

J L Chalmers
GRANDMA !!

Parent signature and comment Rebecca has worked extremely hard and consistently to achieve a high degree of success. I am very proud of her efforts which got an "A" class result. Well done. Ditto! gr

Samples from Rebecca's book study assessment.

Peer comments

Student's name: ....

Date: ....

Class member's name	Check	Class member's comment

The peer-comment sheet used to gather student responses to each book study oral presentation.

Great calm-a-rama. You spoke clearly.
Good speech and Presentation
Well done. I really liked your Clam-a-rama
I loved the Calm-a-rama :
love the calm-a-rama, spoke clearly, well prepared
calm-a-rama great lot of work done, good time managment

Good models but you need to speakup

A fab presentation, spoke clearly
The calm-arama was magnificent
Great model and very creative
Great work and well done.
The calm-arama was great
excellent speeches, marvellous
excellent confidence, great clear voice

Sensational work, excellent.
Interesting and well prepared, you could have spoken louder
Great Illustrations and Well Presented.
Excellent presentation
The models were pretty cool!
I enjoyed watching & listening to it!
You made a mask and a half.
I liked your calm-a-rama you had neat work

Loved the calm-a-rama, organised + great presentation
The Illustrations were good.
very well prepared. ✓
The carmarama was good
very, very welldone, loved the carmarama

Peer comments on Rebecca's oral presentation, which included her draft design for a 'calm-a-rama' (below).

Draft Design for the Invention called: The Calm-a-rama
Tube
container sented balls
batteries
radio head phones.
It is a radio which has calm sounds and a smelling masks it help people calm down the calm-a-rama way!

References

Bloom, B (1956) *Taxonomy of Educational Objectives: The Classification of Educational Goals*. Longmans, London.

Wiederhold, C with Kagan, S (1995) *Cooperative Learning and Higher Level Thinking: The Q-matrix*. Kagan Cooperative Learning, San Juan Capistrano, California.

term four

Chapter 6: Media texts

Planning

The last term of this year-long program does not entail a major assignment, but involves the study of a variety of media texts. Included are texts sourced from magazines, television and newspapers. Study is broken into discrete units, each one conducted over several weeks.

Spoken, written and visual texts are part of our everyday lives. They are presented to us in comics, billboards, magazines and newspapers. They are delivered electronically via radio, television and the Internet. They inform us, control us, direct us and persuade us. They are part of the way that our world shapes us, and part of what creates our view of ourselves in society. People in our community constantly draw upon media texts as a source of information and entertainment, and these texts shape our knowledge, opinions and attitudes.

For these reasons, media texts should be part of students' learning in their reading. Students should be enabled to access and benefit from the content of media texts; at the same time, they should be aware of the ways in which they are being positioned — perhaps manipulated — by the authors of these texts. As Allan Luke says: "Literacy education is about the distribution of knowledge and power in contemporary society".

Another important part of the term's work is reading novels for enjoyment. Since the students have worked in great depth to understand and appreciate novels, I encourage them to continue reading for enjoyment. Sustained silent reading is a small, but enjoyable, part of at least three days per week.

All of my students are expected to have a novel to read during this time. I regularly provide brief periods for sharing a really good book, and I continue to recommend books that I have just read or heard about. Students continue to record their reading on their computer database; this is included in their portfolio at the end of the year.

The major investigations of media texts deal with:

◆ stereotyping

◆ point of view

◆ targeted audiences

◆ inclusion and exclusion

◆ purpose

◆ content analysis.

The media sources investigated are:

◆ magazines

◆ television advertisements

◆ newspapers.

Targeted outcomes

The outcomes expected from this group of units are very different from those previously targeted. Students:

◆ recognise stereotyping and make personal judgements about its appropriateness

◆ recognise the 'silences' in text, and demonstrate an awareness of what is excluded from a text, as well as what is included

◆ understand that writers have a target audience in mind, and that this means some people are excluded from texts

◆ question what they hear and read, and are able to value different interpretations of the same text

◆ develop an awareness that there are many ways of reading or viewing a text, and that different people may have different points of view about the same text

◆ recognise that different text types have different purposes, and that purpose is a major determining aspect of how a text will be constructed

◆ appreciate that language is a powerful tool, and that the language of power can be used in many different ways.

These outcomes focus on the Contextual Understandings strand of the national English statement and profile.

Magazines (3 weeks)

By the time they reach Year 6, students are able to see that they form part of an audience that may be targeted by magazine writers. However, not all students are aware that they may be manipulated by the articles, advertising, competitions and visual elements in magazines. This unit aims to develop this awareness.

Selecting magazines to study

There are many criteria that could be used to locate and select magazines for classroom study. I have found that it is useful, when sharing questions and insights, for the whole class to be working with magazines that target a similar audience. Three typical foci are:

- magazines that have a targeted audience that does not include the students — each student has a copy of the same publication

- magazines that have a targeted audience that does include the students — each student has a copy of the same publication

- magazines that have a targeted audience that includes the students' age group, but represent different interests — each student has a magazine, but groups within the class have different magazines representing the different interests, eg music, hobbies, sport.

In the latter case, I suggest that students in a given group share the same publication.

It is often difficult for middle-years students to recognise the manipulation techniques that magazines use when the students' age group is exclusively targeted. For this reason, it is helpful to consider a magazine that targets an audience from a different age group, such as women. The *Women's Weekly* is a good choice, as the format and targeted audience are familiar.

If students are considering magazines aimed at their own age group, be prepared for them to experience difficulty in recognising stereotyping or narrow representation. Bear in mind, though, that students' interests are engaged fully when they work with texts that they enjoy; they are usually very willing to buy such texts if asked. Negotiating the particular magazine that will be considered by each group is the first step in creating awareness of a targeted audience. Students often choose something along the lines of *TV Hits*, which works well in these lessons and is read by both boys and girls.

Parents who may have concerns about their child buying one of these magazines are usually brought on side when I explain that it is being done to counteract manipulation, which is generally their main objection.

Whichever way a magazine may be chosen, I bring a further selection so that samples targeting a wide variety of audiences can be demonstrated. I try to provide magazines that target such audiences as women, men, computer enthusiasts, craftspersons, children, gardeners, car enthusiasts, games players, collectors and sportspeople. Many other interests are catered for by the magazine trade.

It is easiest to conduct this series of lessons if each student has his or her own magazine. This needs to be organised, either by asking each student to buy it, or by budgeting for this expense at the beginning of the year. Most students are able to purchase their own, but be sensitive to those who are unable to do so, and be prepared to cover this number out of school resources.

Lesson 1: Investigating the selected magazine

First, the class jointly considers the selected magazine/s, discussing its appeal. The following questions can help to focus this discussion.

- What do you like about this magazine?

- What do you dislike?

- Who do you think would buy this publication?

- Which people in the photographs are familiar to you?

The discussion gives the class a shared understanding of who knows and likes the magazine and who is unfamiliar with it or does not like it.

Some questions that require students to consider their parents'/carers' likely response to the magazine can develop further understanding. For example:

- What would parents think about this magazine being read by their children?

- What would parents think about reading this magazine for themselves?

- Are there some differences because people are different ages? What are they?

The class reaches a collective understanding of what students like and dislike about the magazine:

- Does everyone feel the same about the magazine?

- What are the differences?

- What are the reasons for the differences?

The findings that emerge are recorded under two columns on a large sheet: 'Positive opinion' and 'Negative opinion'. The sheet is posted for further reference.

Lesson 2: Identifying differences in format

By discussing the features of the chosen magazine, students will develop further insight, and a vocabulary to use in future discussions.

Students begin with group discussions — I use the students' collaborative learning groups. The groups consider the following focus questions.

- How would you describe the layout that this magazine uses?

- How big are the chunks of text?

- What type of pictures and illustrations are included?

- How are headings presented?

- What general area is covered by words and images?

- What specific topics does the magazine cover?

- How does the magazine use colour?

- How much of the magazine contains advertising?

These questions focus students' attention on how the publication is made up. Each group reports back, and the responses are recorded.

From these observations, the following questions for the whole class group flow easily.

◆ Why did the editors and designers choose these features?

◆ What other magazines have a similar layout?

◆ What magazines do you know that are laid out differently?

◆ What things do editors and designers consider when they decide on a particular style of layout?

Students consolidate their thinking and learning by completing a further activity. Using their reading book, they use diagrams to illustrate magazine layout styles that have been recognised. They identify the features of each style, using labels to annotate their diagrams.

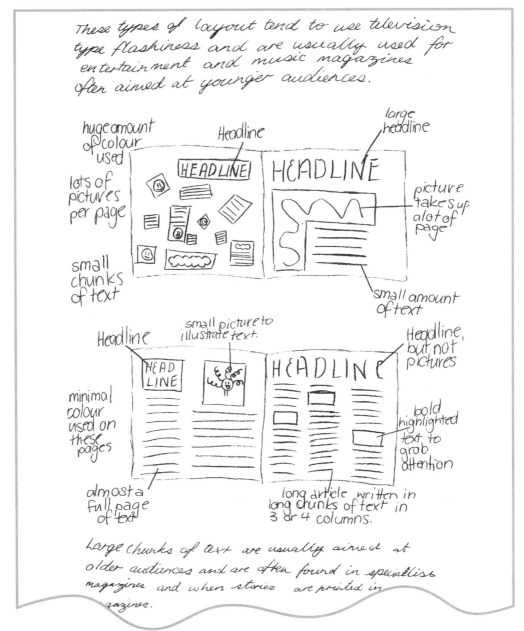

Stephanie's annotated diagrams identifying two distinct styles of magazine layout.

An Explicit Reading Program

Lesson 3: Focus on stereotypes

With the class now familiar with different magazine formats, students begin an investigation of gender and cultural stereotypes.

As a class, students discuss what 'stereotype' means, and reach a conclusion. For example, a stereotype:

◆ generalises typical observations from the past

◆ is built up over time

◆ refers to people, places and situations.

Once the class agrees on a definition and records it for posting in the classroom, students survey the illustrations in their magazine to discover:

◆ how many men are represented

◆ how many women are represented

◆ how many different cultures are represented

◆ what body and skin types are represented

◆ what the people from these groups are shown to be doing.

Note that our understanding of 'culture' is being continuously reshaped. While the idea of identifying 'cultures' by observing images presents its own set of questions, culture remains an important concept to apply when considering dominant/absent representations and perspectives. Students might well benefit from whole-class clarification of this term before completing the above activity. This discussion could include the notion of 'subculture', or culture within culture.

Students record their survey results in tabular format in their reading book. (My students are familiar with conducting surveys and recording their tallied data in this way.)

Lesson 4: Magazines and reality

The whole class reviews the information collated in lesson 3. Together, the students reach consensus about how the magazine represents the different gender and cultural groups. Their discussion could focus on:

◆ gender: How many men? How many women? What are they doing? What are they not doing? What are they wearing? Are both groups represented fairly? Can you identify any gender stereotypes? What are they?

◆ culture: How many cultural groups are represented? How many in each group? How are they depicted? Does this reflect Australian society? Can you identify any cultural stereotypes? What are they?

The students then form small groups to discuss the following questions.

◆ Compare the picture of life represented in the magazine to the way you understand real life. How much of the magazine shows things as they really are? How much is inaccurate, or made up?

◆ How does the magazine's representation of life compare to your own life?

Each group reports back. The class then develops consensus-based responses to the questions above. These are recorded and posted in the classroom.

Lessons 5 and 6: Targeted audience

As a class, students identify the features of a magazine cover. Each student then selects a target audience and creates a magazine cover aimed at appealing to that audience. Students may use a computer, cut out pictures, or develop their own artwork. A homework session may be needed to complete this task.

The covers are displayed around the classroom. A 'Magazine cover' feedback sheet, with room for five responses, is attached to each display. The students are asked to give feedback on five different class members' work, commenting positively about particular features:

Magazine cover

Student response sheet

Comment about one feature of this cover, saying how it appeals to a targeted audience.

Name	Comment

Lesson 7: Portfolio assessment

This task builds on lesson 4, developing individual understanding of stereotyping and providing a vehicle for assessing this understanding.

The students select a stereotype of gender or culture that they have identified from their magazine. Each creates a collage of magazine cut-outs (text and/or pictures) showing the way that this stereotype is depicted in the magazine. They include a caption that explains how the publication is representing people from that cultural or gender group.

When completed, the collages are displayed in the classroom.

Lesson 8: Who is missing?

One way in which a group may be stereotyped is to include only members of that group who have a restricted range of attributes, omitting those who do not have these attributes. The following exercise leads students to recognise the many types of people not represented by particular magazines.

Students form pairs. Each pair considers a magazine picture — this may be the same photocopied picture for everyone, although I sometimes supply a different picture for each student pair. I then provide each pair with the following pro forma, on which they base their discussion and responses.

Magazine pictures

Name: ....

Name: ....

With your background knowledge of stereotyping, what can you say about this picture? Refer to the following questions.

What cultures are represented? ....

....

What genders are represented? ....

....

Who is missing? ....

....

Why? ....

....

How would these people feel if they were always excluded? ....

....

Do you think anything should be changed? ....

Why do you say that? ....

....

What other comments can you make about this picture? ....

....

....

....

....

Each pair reports back to the class group, presenting their findings.

To consolidate their learning about magazines, students complete a review sheet that becomes part of their portfolio.

Magazine review

Name: ....

In this unit I have learnt:

• ....

• ....

about magazines,

• ....

• ....

about targeted audiences, and

• ....

• ....

about stereotypes.

Write your opinion about the ways in which magazines stereotype gender or culture.

....

....

....

....

....

An Explicit Reading Program

Television advertisements (3 weeks)

Television advertisements capture students' imagination. Catchy advertisements stick relentlessly in the minds of adults. All of us get mightily tired of them as they are repeated over and over.

The presence of advertisements is one of the reasons for a few families choosing not to have television in their homes, and explains why many more watch only the ABC. However, advertisements are watched repeatedly by the great majority of our society, and need to be investigated if students are to cope intelligently with the lifelong exposure that they will have to these electronic texts.

Selecting an advertisement to study

There is an unlimited, ever-changing supply of advertisements from which to choose. However, choosing the right one is not always as easy as it may seem. The following considerations can guide the decision.

◆ The advertisements should be about products that will interest the students.

◆ The advertisements should promote a product or service easily identifiable to the students, and about which they have some knowledge.

◆ The advertisements should not contain issues, products or services that parents may find contentious.

◆ The characters may be stereotyped or shown in non-traditional roles: you may prefer discussion on one or the other.

◆ Humour can add to the students' enjoyment.

◆ Animals provide appeal for many students.

◆ If the advertisement is one of a series, you may need to include others in the series.

I tape the selected advertisement several times onto one videotape to allow repeated viewing without rewinding. This can take a little longer than expected; not only is it tricky to catch the beginning, but my experience is that, having decided upon which ad to tape and put aside a viewing night to record it, that particular ad is not shown. Plan ahead!

Lesson 1: Familiarisation

The class views the taped advertisement several times. It is helpful to view the ad with and without sound, so that students can focus on different aspects.

Students then fill out the following focusing sheet, 'Television advertisement', which was developed using elements drawn from the Wiederhold question matrix (see also pp 18 and 73).

Television advertisement: Focusing sheet

What is being advertised?

....

Where is the advertisement set?

....

Why?

....

....

When does the action take place?

....

What style of music is being played?

....

Why?

....

....

Who is most important in the advertisement?

....

Why?

....

....

Is the advertisement appealing?

....

Why?

....

....

How does the advertisement get its message to the audience?

....

....

....

....

4. Which music is being played?

   Jazz music.

   Why? *to capture cheerfulness, in spite of the weather.*

5. Who is most important in the advertisement?

   The newly married couple.

   Why? *Because they have a special reason to take photos.*

6. Why is the advertisement so appealing?

   Because the young couple managed to take their honeymoon photos, even though it rained all the time. One feels sorry for the young couple, but pleased that they were still able to have fun and enjoy themselves through the rain.

7. How does the advertisement get its message to the audience?

   By showing most unfavourable weather in which to take photos then keeps our interest by including a young, attractive who over-come all weather odds and still have great fun.

A sample from Stephanie's response to the 'Television advertisement' focusing sheet.

Once the students have completed the focusing sheet, they form groups of three or four to discuss the questions:

◆ Which audience would this advertisement appeal to most?

◆ Give reasons why this ad would succeed or not succeed in capturing the attention of prospective customers.

◆ Which part is a viewer likely to take away with them to think about?

The groups report back to the class, which then jointly decides on answers to the following questions.

◆ Is this a successful advertisement?

◆ What makes it successful?

◆ How could it be improved?

Lesson 2: 'Six-hat' thinking

The class group watches the chosen advertisement again before forming small groups. Each group is allocated one hat colour — a different colour for each group (see also p 17).

Each group is given the task sheet for its hat (see below). Before the groups set to work, someone in each group reads out their questions and task. The groups then record their impressions of the advertisement from the point of view signified by their hat colour.

Students may need a quick refresher about the type of thinking represented by each colour hat. If your students have had no experience with this model, you will need to explain and model the thinking approaches signified by each hat.

Television advertisement: 'Six-hat' thinking

Black hat

(Checks for weaknesses, logic and evidence; makes statements.)

- What claim is made?

- What evidence is given?

- Who is not represented?

- Would the product or service always perform as claimed?

- Who is the targeted audience? Does the ad target a wide enough audience?

- Are there other audiences who might be targeted by this product?

Present your findings on a large sheet of paper for display.

Television advertisement: 'Six-hat' thinking

Yellow hat

(Finds the good points — the benefits, the reasons why it will work.)

- What are the benefits of this product?

- Who benefits from this product?

- What is the appeal of this ad?

- How do the sound and pictures work together?

- What does the ad do to get its message across to the audience?

Explain your findings on a large sheet of paper for display.

Television advertisement: 'Six-hat' thinking

White hat

(What information do we have? What information do we need, and how do we get it?)

- What do we learn about the product from this ad?
- How is this presented?
- Whose point of view are we getting?
- What other information do we need about the product to make an informed choice?
- How could we get more information?

Explain your findings on a large sheet of paper for display.

Television advertisement: 'Six-hat' thinking

Green hat

(Uses creativity to generate new ideas and suggest improvements.)

- How could the advertisement be improved?
- How could the product be improved?
- What other audiences could be targeted?
- How would you change the ad to target other audiences?

Explain your findings on a large sheet of paper for display.

Television advertisement: 'Six-hat' thinking

Red hat

(Sets out feelings, emotions and hunches.)

- What feelings does this ad evoke for you?
- What different feelings might this ad evoke with different audiences, eg men, women, girls, boys, teenagers, elderly people, people from different cultures?

In table form, present your findings for display in the classroom.

Television advertisement: 'Six-hat' thinking

Blue hat

(Defines the focus, purpose and plans; decides steps.)

- Identify and list the different sections of the ad, in sequence.
- Draw a picture board of the sequence and label each picture with what you consider to be the advertiser's purpose for that section.

Present the picture board on a large sheet of paper for display in the classroom.

Lesson 3: Ad types

Student groups report on their findings from the six-hat thinking task, explaining their large-format presentations. A display is mounted in the classroom.

As a class, students then discuss the different types of advertisements seen on television, and make a chart for posting in the classroom. The types identified may include:

- story
- jingle
- bad taste
- spruiking
- cut price
- expert recommendation
- celebrity endorsement
- glamour
- humour
- nature/health
- any others your class may identify.

In pairs, students consider the question: 'How do different types of advertisements appeal to different audiences?'

The pairs report back. The whole class then discusses the question: 'What types appeal most to our class group?'

Homework

Students are asked to watch an ad that appeals to them. They identify a range of features prompted by the 'Ad watching' pro forma (over), which they complete.

Ad watching

Name: ....

1. What is being advertised?

2. What is the purpose of the ad?

    To inform   [ ]

    To explain   [ ]

    To coerce   [ ]

    To catch attention by being different   [ ]

    ....   [ ]

    ....   [ ]

    ....   [ ]

3. What information is being given by this ad?

    ....

    ....

4. What music is being used?

    ....

    How does it add to the advertisement?

    ....

    ....

5. Do you consider this ad is appropriate for the product? Explain.

    ....

    ....

    ....

    ....

6. Is the message of the advertisement clear, or are there distractions? Explain.

    ....

    ....

    ....

    ....

7. What type of advertisement would you call this?

    ....

Lesson 4: Writing an advertisement for performance

Dramatisations scripted and performed by groups of students are powerful learning constructs. They involve negotiation, cooperation, written and oral language refinement, problem-solving and performance. They integrate all strands of the English curriculum.

Since the genre being developed here is a television advertisement, it is preferable to record students' performances on video. Each group is then able to review the development and presentation of its ad. However, the final presentation could simply be a performance for the class or a wider school audience.

When explaining the task to the class, make the time frame clear and remind the students of the need for careful time management. It is also worthwhile to discuss the need for cooperative group skills. If these skills have been developed previously, this will be a simple reminder. If not, it will be necessary to explain, reflect on and monitor cooperative skills such as organisation, respect, turn-taking, role responsibility, goal-setting, decision-making etc.

In groups of four or five, students:

◆ decide on a product to advertise

◆ decide on the type of advertisement to present

◆ write the advertisement

◆ decide on the sound to use.

At the end of the lesson, groups report on their progress. A fully developed piece of writing is not required here — notes that are understood by the group are sufficient. Groups may choose to record in a variety of ways, for example a brief script, a storyboard or notes.

Lessons 5 and 6: Rehearsal

Students jointly discuss the criteria set out in 'Television advertisements: Unit assessment' (see p 112). These criteria are displayed in the classroom. In their groups, the students:

◆ put the finishing touches to their scripts/storyboards

◆ identify and organise the cast, director (if needed) and other resources required to perform the advertisement

◆ rehearse for a performance.

Lessons 7 and 8: Performance

Each group performs its advertisement for the class. If possible, it is videotaped by a person with expertise in this area. If there is time, it is valuable for groups to receive support and feedback from the class and teacher before the performance is recorded.

Lesson 9: Video-watching

The class watches each video clip, making a collaborative assessment with the teacher: I manage students' feedback as a class discussion, recording it on the 'Advertisement presentation' sheet (opposite). This sheet is copied so that each group member can put one in their portfolio.

I also complete the 'Television advertisements: Unit assessment' sheet for each student. This needs to be completed soon after each performance; the video-watching assists this assessment. I also encourage students to reflect on their learning by completing a 'Television advertisements: Student reflection' sheet (p 113) as homework. All three sheets go home in the student portfolio. If I am able to organise multiple copies of the video, I also send these home to students' families.

Advertisement presentation

Names: ....

Task

With a group, write and present a television advertisement. Make sure you make clear what is being advertised, what type of advertisement this is, and which audience you are targeting. Viewers will be asked to comment on the appeal of your ad and on the music or sound that you use.

Assessment

What is being advertised? ....

What type of advertisement is this? ....

Who is the targeted audience? ....

What is the appeal of the advertisement? ....

....

In what way does music or sound add to the advertisement? ....

....

Class comment:

Teacher comment:

Student comment:

Parent comment:

Television advertisements: Unit assessment

Outcomes

The student:

	Poor	Satisfactory	Excellent
speaks with understanding of character, mood and setting			
speaks to an audience with confidence			
portrays a character appropriately for the setting			
speaks within the genre of television advertisement			
speaks and performs for recording on video			
speaks fluently and with expression			
shows an understanding of stereotypes			
works cooperatively in groups			
manages time competently.			

- speaks with understanding of character, mood and setting
- speaks to an audience with confidence
- portrays a character appropriately for the setting
- speaks within the genre of television advertisement
- speaks and performs for recording on video
- speaks fluently and with expression
- shows an understanding of stereotypes
- works cooperatively in groups
- manages time competently.

Student comment:

Teacher comment:

Parent comment:

Television advertisements: Student reflection

Name: ....

What did I learn about advertisements on television?

Appeal

Purpose

Information

Action

Further comment:

Parent signature:

Newspapers (2 weeks)

By now, the students should have a good understanding of targeted audiences, stereotypes, missing groups, appeal and text purpose. Having studied magazines that target a particular audience and advertisements that incorporate a wider audience, students now move on to newspapers. In the newspapers studied here, the aim of the publishers is to include a wide audience; an understanding of this, along with a deeper comprehension of media texts, forms the broad aim of this unit.

Lesson 1: Who is in the newspaper, and who isn't?

Very often, newspapers exclude women's sport and its personalities from the sporting pages. While there are various reasons for this, the discrepancy provides an excellent focus for data-gathering and discussion.

I use the first lesson as an introduction to newspapers, building on the knowledge of stereotypes developed in the previous units.

Students are asked to bring a newspaper from home on a particular day. I provide some extras, as some students are unable to supply a copy. One newspaper between two or three usually works well. I join the class in looking through the sports section, then guide a discussion about:

- the way the section is structured

- the sports that are represented

- the representation of men and women in the photographs

- the readership of the section.

The class then surveys the sports section of a mass-circulation newspaper for a week, recording: the number of people of each sex in photographs; the sports they are involved in; and the activity they are doing. For example, one photo might contain: men; involved in AFL football; and marking the ball. Another photo might show: a woman; involved in netball; and posing with a child. This survey works best if each student has a paper every day; if this is not possible, one paper per pair or group, or even one paper for the whole class, can work.

The table opposite provides a useful way to record the required information. It would need to be drawn to a larger scale if it were used with the whole class.

Day	Gender	Tally	Total number	Sports	Activities
Monday	Men				
	Women				
Tuesday	Men				
	Women				
Wednesday	Men				
	Women				
Thursday	Men				
	Women				
Friday	Men				
	Women				
Saturday	Men				
	Women				
Totals	Men				
	Women				

I explain the task of surveying the paper and prepare students for the data-collection requirement. The survey results can be recorded: as part of related mathematics activities; in students' reading books; and/or on a large-format chart on the classroom wall. It must be decided in advance whether to count every man and every woman, or whether a photograph containing men or women is counted as one. At the beginning of the following week, students add their tallies for each day, producing a final survey total and report in lesson 4. In the meantime, they complete lessons 2 and 3.

Lesson 2: Different sections for different audiences

Students do not always know all the sections of the newspaper. Often, they are unaware of the wide-ranging audiences that the different sections target.

In this lesson, groups are asked to go through the paper, listing the sections that they can find and the pages that these sections start on. When finished, the groups report back, and their suggestions are collated into a class list. The list might include the following:

◆ News
  – Local
  – National
  – International

- ◆ Finance
- ◆ Entertainment
- ◆ Amusements
  - – Comics
  - – Crossword/Puzzles
- ◆ Letters to the editor
- ◆ Editorial
- ◆ Sport
- ◆ Television
- ◆ Weather
- ◆ Classified ads
- ◆ Features — in-depth discussion of news or issues
- ◆ Computing
- ◆ Arts — books, theatre, films
- ◆ Travel
- ◆ Magazine.

Each student group is allocated a character (see under), and is asked to identify the sections of the newspaper that that character might be most interested in.

Character cards

Marco is a 24-year-old man who has just finished university. He has a new job in the country and now needs to buy a car. The car must be reliable, but he cannot spend more than $7000 to buy it.

Ian is an accountant who needs to keep up with share trading, and is very interested in the financial happenings in Australia and around the world. Ian and his partner like to eat out, and they are planning an overseas trip in the near future.

Michael is a student who is very interested in computers. His parents need to update their computer and, because of his expertise, he has been asked to help in deciding what to buy and where to get the best deal. Michael has a great sense of humour and likes to go to movies when he has enough money. He also likes pop music and his CD collection is growing, but not as fast as he would like.

Margaret is a grandmother who has lived all her life in the same city. She is interested in what is happening in the city and around the state. She likes to keep up with the news. Because she is getting older, she wants to keep up with who has died as well as which of her many friends are having grandchildren. She likes shopping, but her pension does not leave her with a great deal of money to spend, so she must choose carefully.

Jane is a busy office worker who needs to keep up with the state news because of her job. She also likes to keep up with the office conversation to show that she is an interesting and knowledgeable person. Jane likes going to discos, but is saving for a car, so does not go out as often as she used to.

Nader works in a school, wants to know what is happening in the world and is interested in cars. He follows a particular football team and always talks about this in the staff room.

Tran is a well-read person who works in a library. She is interested in books and music, and likes to attend films and concerts. She is interested in happenings throughout the world and is interested to hear other people's comments and views. She often writes to the newspaper to express her own views.

Andrew is a bicycle rider in his late 20s. He is committed to conserving the environment, and does all he can to reduce pollution and waste. He disposes of his rubbish responsibly and wants others to understand the benefits of re-using and recycling materials. He often writes to newspapers on this topic. Andrew's sporting interests include bike-riding, bushwalking and swimming.

Anna is a teenager. School takes up lots of her time. She plays netball and belongs to a swimming club, where she won the club championship last year. She likes going to movies and shopping with her friends. Her CD collection is growing, but pocket money does not allow her to buy very many and she must choose carefully.

The groups report back to the class, explaining why they have chosen particular sections for their character. Other class members are invited to provide different points of view and ideas.

It is valuable to reflect on this activity in the light of previous learning about stereotypes. Students may consider and discuss whether their character represents a stereotype, and whether it is likely that newspaper writers and editors use stereotypes as a way of identifying a target audience.

Lesson 3: Different papers for different audiences

The other way that the media industry targets a variety of audiences is to produce different types of newspapers, each with a particular audience in mind. Not all students are aware of this variety, so I bring a range of newspapers for viewing. Some that might be used (and their audience bases) are:

◆ *The Australian* (national)

◆ *Financial Review* (business/finance sector)

◆ *The Advertiser* (state)

- *The Messenger* (local area)
- *Adelaide Review* (city/visitor)
- *Rip It Up* (street)
- *On Dit* (university).

In groups, students are given one paper to browse and discuss. Each group then lists the sections included in its paper and writes a characterisation for a person they feel might be a reader of this type of paper.

Groups report back to the class, showing the sections they have identified, explaining the types of articles contained and reading out the characterisation that they have prepared.

Lesson 4: Who is in the newspaper, and who isn't? Survey results

Students collate their survey tallies and make comparisons. Because of varying interpretations, some differences will occur, but an overall picture will emerge. Typically, around 85% of pictures represent men and 15% represent women (although no doubt each class will arrive at different percentages according to the newspaper and sport). I prompt a discussion of these statistics with questions such as:

- What is your opinion of this representation?
- Why do you think there might be this discrepancy?
- Do you think it should be changed?

This can promote some heated discussion; some will favour the status quo, while others will be offended and will suggest change. At this point, an 'opinion line' (in which students position themselves on a continuum of agreement with a proposition) provides an excellent illustration of where class opinion is spread. This allows me to point out that, like the class, readers are of many different opinions.

In the next part of the lesson, groups form to discuss the other statistics collected. This is focused around questions such as:

- What different sports are reported about?
- Which sports are left out?
- Why do you think this is so?
- Would you recommend change? What change?
- What are the majority of men doing in the photographs?
- What are the majority of women doing?
- What are the differences? Do you think these differences exist because of the choices made by the photographers and editors? Do their choices need to be changed?

The groups report back to the class and a chart of opinions is made to facilitate whole-class discussion. Jointly, the class reaches a conclusion about:

◆ the coverage of different sports

◆ the ways in which women and men are represented.

Lessons 5 and 6: Newspaper articles — comprehension

For this lesson, I choose eight newspaper articles containing topics that students are familiar with. Finding suitable articles may take some time: skim-reading of the articles will not be sufficient to ensure that the students have the necessary prior knowledge for understanding.

I select articles that:

◆ contain words that are familiar to the students

◆ have concepts that are readily understood

◆ will not cause any dissension among the parents

◆ are interesting to the students

◆ are long enough to contain some depth of comment, but not so long that students are daunted by the volume of reading

◆ do not demand specific prior knowledge that the students may not possess.

I find that I need to read very carefully to ensure all of these criteria are met. It is easy to glance briefly at an article, say, on sport, and miss quite difficult concepts or the fact that prior knowledge is needed.

In groups of four, students use an article and Bloom's taxonomy of questioning (as used in the term 3 reading assignment, pp 77–78, but changed slightly to cater for this task) to set questions, all of which require written answers. The 'Question-setting for a newspaper article' matrix (see over) is given to each student and is carefully explained using a model article and set of questions.

Twelve questions must be set — two from each section of the taxonomy, ensuring that students demonstrate in-depth analysis of the article.
(I check the questions carefully to ensure that they can be answered, and to ascertain the group's understanding of the article.)

Once the questions have been set and I have checked them, they are passed on to another group, which selects six to answer. The answers are returned to the question-setting group, which assesses and comments on them.

When the questions have been answered, assessed and commented upon, the responses are displayed in the classroom for the teacher and class to look at. This activity produces two pieces of work that demonstrate comprehension and analysis — the questions set and the answers given.

A Year in Texts

Question-setting for a newspaper article

Name: ....

Group 1: Set twelve questions or tasks, two from each section, then hand these on to the next group to answer.

	Useful verbs		Question/Task suggestions	Questions/Tasks
Knowledge	Tell Locate Name Write	Describe Find List State	List main events. Make a timeline. Compile a fact chart. Draw a table of information.	• • • •
Comprehension	Explain Interpret Discuss Compare	Predict Outline Describe	Illustrate an event. Write in your own words …. Describe activities, places or people. Explain the differences between …. Note the most important points. Describe where the action takes place.	• • • • •
Application	Solve Use Calculate Classify	Illustrate Examine Show	Calculate something that is provided in numerical terms. Develop a set of instructions. Identify the issues raised.	• • •
Analysis	Distinguish Compare Categorise Advertise	Contrast Explain Examine	Make a poster to advertise something from the article. Identify the main issue, and suggest how improvements could be made. Examine the reasons for what has happened.	• • •
Synthesis	Create Compose Plan Design	Improve Propose Predict	Identify the issues and suggest how improvements could be made. Compose a poem about the issues. Propose another way of dealing with the problem. Design a helpful machine to deal with the problem or issue described. Prepare a set of criteria for something from the article.	• • • • •
Evaluation	Select Judge Choose Recommend	Discuss Decide	Develop a better solution for the problem or issue. Suggest a better way to manage the problem or issue. Write a letter about the problem or issue. Prepare a list of rules and say why they are appropriate.	• • • •

Group 2: Choose six of the questions/tasks, one from each section. Complete each one as fully as possible. Make your meanings as clear as possible. Pass your responses back to group 1 for assessment and comment.

THREE-YEAR-OLD CENTRE WINS STATE ENVIRONMENT PRIZE

Students dip into life under the waves

By BEN HOOPER

A HENLEY Beach centre where primary school students are educated about the marine world has won a major environment award.

The Marine Discovery Centre at the Star of the Sea School won the South Australian section of the Readers Digest Environment Awards 2000.

The award carries a $2500 cash prize. Established three years ago, the centre attracts more than 5000 visiting students annually. It is now in the running for one of three national prizes worth up to $15,000 to be announced on October 29.

"We are booked about a year ahead," the centre's project officer, Tim Hoile, said yesterday.

"It was my dream to set it up – I have a passion for the marine environment.

"Our marine life is suffering and through community action and education we can make a huge difference."

Students who visit the centre – the first primary school learning centre of its type in Australia – are taught about local marine life and ways to protect it.

The centre houses four large aquariums containing various forms of marine life, including a one-year-old Port Jackson shark which was hatched at the centre, seahorses and schools of local fish.

Visitors to the centre are also taken on a marine discovery trail along the nearby beach.

Students from the Star of the Sea School, adjacent to the centre, contribute to its displays and also help monitor the marine life on show.

"The students are very enthusiastic in their support of the centre," Mr Hoile said.

"They really love the video microscope (which allows users to peer closely inside an aquarium) and the marine trail walk along the beach."

Mr Hoile said the $2500 prize would help fund future plans to install video conferencing facilities, an e-mail service and a "gulf-cam" offering views of St Vincent Gulf on the marine centre's website.

A model article used to develop sample questions/tasks (over) through the application of Bloom's taxonomy (opposite).
Source: Ben Hooper, The Advertiser, *Sunday 7 October 2000.*

Modelled questions

- ◆ Knowledge
  - – Where is the Marine Discovery Centre located?
  - – What will the $2500 prize money be used for?

- ◆ Comprehension
  - – Describe the activities that students can take part in at the Marine Discovery Centre.
  - – When learning about the sea, what is the biggest difference between working in the Marine Discovery Centre and working in an ordinary classroom?

- ◆ Application
  - – Mr Hoile has listed three things that the $2500 prize money might be spent on. If all three were purchased, calculate how much money could be allocated to each one.
  - – Develop a set of behaviour rules for students visiting this discovery centre.

- ◆ Analysis
  - – Why do you think Mr Hoile has a passion for the marine environment?
  - – Make a rough draft of a poster to advertise the Marine Discovery Centre to schools.

- ◆ Synthesis
  - – How might Mr Hoile have funded the future plans for the centre without winning the prize money?
  - – Write a poem about marine life.

- ◆ Evaluation
  - – Write a letter to Mr Hoile, congratulating him on winning the $2500 prize money, and giving reasons why you think that setting up the Marine Discovery Centre was a really good idea.
  - – Does the headline give the reader sufficient information about the article? Explain.

References

Australian Women's Weekly. Monthly magazine. Australian Consolidated Press, Sydney.

De Bono, E (1988) *Six Thinking Hats*. In *Masterthinker 11* (kit). International Center for Creative Thinking, New York.

TV Hits. Monthly magazine. Pacific Publications, Sydney.

Wiederhold, C with Kagan, S (1995) *Cooperative Learning and Higher Level Thinking: The Q-matrix*. Kagan Cooperative Learning, San Juan Capistrano, California.

Afterword: Reflection and next steps

At the end of the year, like most teachers, I heave a huge sigh of relief that we have managed to get through the usual hectic program of a middle-years classroom.

The assignments and marking have been completed, the reports sent home and the celebratory parties are in full swing — not the time for in-depth reflection!

However, once the new year looms onto the horizon, reflection and planning go hand in hand to make teaching a cyclical practice.

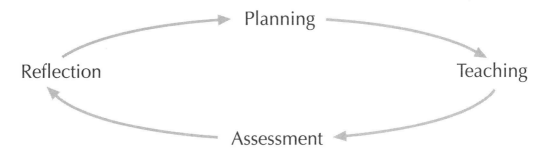

At the beginning of each year, I look back over the previous year's work and reflect on the outcomes achieved by the students I have taught. From this, a number of questions emerge that will influence the coming year's program:

◆ How did the program that I developed and negotiated with my class work for us?

◆ Do I need to reconsider some of the outcomes as I plan for the coming year?

◆ Are there shared themes that can be built upon?

◆ What structural, operational or policy developments at the school will I need to take into account?

◆ What updates will I need to make to incorporate my own new learnings, or to further develop parts of the program?

◆ How can I streamline the assessment of my class?

◆ How can I include collaborative and cooperative work to build on these skills?

◆ Have I taken essential learnings and key competencies into account so that students are prepared for their future needs?

While this book has outlined the lessons on which my reading program is built, each year sees changes to a variety of activities. Each assignment is developed further to accommodate the needs of a new set of students and a new set of interactions with my colleagues.

I encourage you to use this program either as it is or — even more so — as a starting point to develop a reading program for your own group of students. I hope that you and your students have a great year, every year, in texts.

Bibliography / Suggested resources

A Statement on English for Australian Schools. Curriculum Corporation, Melbourne, 1994.

Australian Women's Weekly. Monthly magazine. Australian Consolidated Press, Sydney.

Baker, J (1991) *Window.* Julia MacRae, London.

Blake, D & Hamilton, E (1995) *Text and Context: A Guide to Speaking and Writing.* Longmans, Melbourne.

Bloom, B (1956) *Taxonomy of Educational Objectives: The Classification of Educational Goals.* Longmans, London.

Burke, K (1996) *How to Assess Authentic Learning.* Hawker Brownlow Education, Melbourne.

Clark, M (1992) *Plastic City.* Random House, Sydney.

Classroom magazine (seven issues yearly). Scholastic Australia, Sydney.

Clement, R (1995) *Just Another Ordinary Day.* Angus & Robertson, Sydney.

Crew, G (1996) *Bright Star.* Lothian Books, Melbourne.

Crew, G (1994) *The Watertower.* Era Publications, SA.

Davies, A et al. (1994) *Together Is Better: Collaborative Assessment, Evaluation and Reporting.* Eleanor Curtain, Melbourne.

De Bono, E (1988) *Six Thinking Hats.* In *Masterthinker 11* (kit). International Center for Creative Thinking, New York.

English: A Curriculum Profile for Australian Schools. Curriculum Corporation, Melbourne, 1994.

Fatchen, M (1980) *The River Kings.* Methuen Children's Books, London.

Freebody, P, Ludwig, C & Gunn, S (1995) *Everyday Literacy Practices in and out of Schools in Low Socio-economic Urban Communities.* Curriculum Corporation, Melbourne.

Freebody, P & Luke, A (1990) '"Literacies" Programmes: Debates and Demands in Cultural Context'. *Prospect* 11.

Freebody, P & Luke, A (1997) *Constructing Critical Literacies: Teaching and Learning Textual Practice.* Allen & Unwin, Sydney.

Gleitzman, M (1996) *Worry Warts.* Pan, Sydney.

Hancock, J (ed.) (1999) *The Explicit Teaching of Reading.* International Reading Association.

Hathorn, L (1994) *Way Home.* Random House, Sydney.

Honey, E (1996) *Don't Pat the Wombat.* Allen & Unwin, Sydney.

Honey, E (1995) *45 & 47 Stella Street: And Everything that Happened.* Allen & Unwin, Sydney.

Janks, H (1993) *Language, Identity and Power.* Hodder & Stoughton in assoc. with Witwatersrand University Press, Johannesburg.

Jorgensen, G (1989) *Crocodile Beat.* Omnibus Books, Adelaide.

Klein, R (1986) *Boss of the Pool.* Omnibus Books in assoc. with Penguin, Adelaide.

Klein, R (1992) *Came Back to Show You I Could Fly.* Narkaling Productions, Perth.

Marchetta, M (1993) *Looking for Alibrandi.* Penguin, Melbourne.

Marsden, J (1993) *Tomorrow, When the War Began.* Pan Macmillan, Sydney.

Martin, R, Badger, L & Comber, B (eds) (1990) *The First Lunar Landing.* Big book. Era Publications, SA.

Mattingley, C (1971) *Windmill at Magpie Creek.* Hodder & Stoughton, Sydney.

McAfee, A & Browne, A (1984) *The Visitors Who Came to Stay.* Hamish Hamilton, London.

Monk, S (1988) *Raw.* Random House Australia, Sydney.

O'Brien, J (1991) *Reading and Writing Years R–3.* Education Department of South Australia, Adelaide.

O'Brien, J (1991) *Reading and Writing Years 4–7.* Education Department of South Australia, Adelaide.

Park, R (1987) *Playing Beatie Bow.* Angus & Robertson, Sydney.

Paris, S, Wixson, K & Palincsar, A (1986) 'Instructional Approaches to Reading Comprehension'. In E Roth Kops (ed.) *Review of Research in Education.* American Educational Research Association, Washington, DC.

Parry, T & Gregory, G (1988) *Designing Brain-compatible Learning.* Hawker Brownlow Education, Melbourne.

Pohl, M (1997) *Teaching Thinking Skills in the Primary Years: A Whole-school Approach.* Hawker Brownlow Education, Melbourne.

Pohl, M (2000) *Learning to Think, Thinking to Learn: Models and Strategies to Develop a Classroom Culture of Thinking.* Hawker Brownlow Education, Melbourne.

Rolton, G (2000) *Using Picture Story Books: A Resource Book for Teachers.* Macmillan Education.

Rubinstein, G (1986) *Space Demons.* Omnibus Books in assoc. with Puffin, Adelaide.

Tan, S (2000) *The Lost Thing.* Lothian Books, Melbourne.

Thiele, C (1978) *Blue Fin.* Rigby, Adelaide.

Thiele, C (1990) *Jodie's Journey.* Walter McVitty Books, Sydney.

Thiele, C (1976) *Storm Boy.* Rigby, Adelaide.

Thiele, C (1981) *The Fire in the Stone.* Puffin, Harmondsworth, UK.

Turner, E (1991) *Seven Little Australians.* Angus & Robertson, Sydney.

TV Hits. Monthly magazine. Pacific Publications, Sydney.

Westwood, P (1995) 'What Should We Be Teaching Explicitly to At-risk Beginning Readers and Writers?' In *Cornerstones,* modules 6 and 7. South Australian Department of Education and Children's Services, Adelaide.

Wheatley, N (1999) *Luke's Way of Looking.* Hodder Headline Australia, Sydney.

Wiederhold, C with Kagan, S (1995) *Cooperative Learning and Higher Level Thinking: The Q-matrix.* Kagan Cooperative Learning, San Juan Capistrano, California.

Winebrenner, S (1992) *Teaching Gifted Kids in the Regular Classroom.* Hawker Brownlow Education, Melbourne.

Wrightson, P (1971) *I Own the Racecourse!* Penguin, Harmondsworth, UK.